MY HUNT
FOR THE
LOST SHIPS
OF HISTORY

TRUE STORIES of the WORLD's SUNKEN TREASURES

**Captain
JOSEPH AMARAL Jr.**

This book is memoir.
The events are portrayed to the best of the author's memory
and present recollections of experiences over time.
No names have been changed, no characters invented,
no events fabricated.
Arnica Press is committed to publishing works of quality and
integrity. In that spirit, we are proud to offer this book to our
readers; however, the story, the experiences,
and the words are the author's alone.

Published by
ARNICA PRESS
www.ArnicaPress.com

Copyright © 2025 Captain Joseph Amaral. Jr.

Written by Captain Joseph Amaral. Jr.

Cover Photo:
Photo of Captain Joseph Amaral Jr. by Arnie Carr
Photo of captain's ring by Doug Ayres

Manufactured in the United States of America

ISBN: 978-1-955354-82-0

All rights reserved. No part of this book may be reproduced
or transmitted in any form or by any means, electronic
or mechanical, including photocopying, recording,
or by any information storage and retrieval system,
without the prior written permission from the Author.
This book may not be AI scraped or utilized in AI processes unless
permission in writing is received by the author.

For my dear friend and Grand Master of the sea,
Harvey Harrington

ACKNOWLEDGMENTS

Every fortunate moment in life is meaningless unless it is shared with those you love.

I am especially grateful to my magnificent wife, Christine. You are my world.

To my remarkable son, Josh, who makes me proud every single day, and to my dearest daughter, Christina.

I have been blessed with the kindest, most loving parents, Rita and Joseph Amaral Sr., who instilled in me the principles of life that made me who I am. I know they are smiling from above while keeping a watchful eye on my family every single minute of every day.

My gratitude to the fabulous Doug Ayres, whose generous contribution of his impressive photographic work to this book is irreplaceable. My thanks to Rob Morris and his marvelous sonar scan images.

I wish to thank Sabrina Mesko and her publishing house Arnica Press for her editing skills, book design and other contributions.

And finally, my deep gratitude to my formidable friend, Arnie Carr, whose big-hearted alliance propelled me through countless exciting adventures, to John Fish, a most reliable and fearless co-warrior at sea, and Rob Morris, a wondrous diving companion on the ground and under the sea.
I am indeed a most fortunate man.

The Spell of the Yukon

*"There's gold, and it's haunting and haunting;
It's luring me on as of old;
Yet it isn't the gold that I'm wanting,
So much as just finding the gold."*

By Robert W. Service, 1907

Table of Contents

Acknowledgments 7
Introduction 13
The marvelous ships 17
The mystery of the sea 29
Becoming a diver 37

My Treasure Hunts

CHAPTER ONE ~
THE JACKPOT
The Captain's ring on the DE BRAAK 49

CHAPTER TWO ~
THE GANGSTER
The unsolved murder on JOHN DWIGHT 97

CHAPTER THREE ~
THE GILDED AGE BEAUTY
The luxurious ALVA 121

CHAPTER FOUR ~
THE FORTUNE HUNTERS
The golden treasure on SS BROTHER JONATHAN 141

CHAPTER FIVE ~
THE HEROES, HAULERS AND ENEMIES OF THE HIGH SEAS

The HEROES
The historic PENDLETON 167
The wings beneath the waves 171

The HAULERS
SEACONNET 177
HENRY ENDICOTT 183
WHITE SQUALL 187
POTTSTOWN 193
MARS 197

The ENEMIES
THE GERMAN SUBMARINE 201

CHAPTER SIX~
THE LEGEND
The formidable knight on L'AUGUSTE 207

Final word 221

About the Author 223

INTRODUCTION

If you have a curiosity about the mysterious treasures of countless shipwrecks from long ago, then this book is for you.

Over the many centuries, millions of shipwrecks occurred, and more often than not, the vessels sank into the depths of the ocean or sea, never to be seen or heard of again. They simply disappeared, and no one actually knew when or where.

What happened to them? Are their remains still there? Most likely, yes.
Will they ever see the light of day? Most probably not.

They shall remain below the sea surface, buried in the seabed for eternity.

Suppose a shipwreck occurred closer to the shore, which presented a few other options. Sometimes the people on land witnessed the wreck or later noticed the sunken vessel, and quite often some remains were found on shore soon thereafter. Closer to our present time, the formidably brave Coast Guards were usually sent into a deadly storm to undertake a dangerous rescue mission and most likely succeeded in saving precious human lives.

There was also a likelihood that other ships nearby were able to observe the dramatic event and, if possible, offer help to rescue whomever they could. And then there was the chance that a few heroic souls made it to the shore on their very own and later shared the harrowing tale of their severe test of endurance and miraculous survival.

As a professional diving expert, I have had exceptional experiences with fascinating old shipwrecks all over the world, so it seems noteworthy to share with you the few that truly stand out and are tightly interwoven with significant historical events.

All treasures or remains of a long-ago shipwreck carry a message, an inspiring idea, or a gem of timeless wisdom to help us appreciate the life here and now. They also revive the old intricate stories of the brave souls who traveled the sea and courageously faced the many risks such daring sea voyages presented.

Ships are closely intertwined with human history and remain an intricate part of helping us fulfil our dreams, longings, and pursuits. They are a monument to the immense courage needed to overcome the dangers of the ocean and travel through the foreboding stormy waves to finally reach a desired destination. Sometimes it does not matter where the travelers landed, for the journey's purpose fulfilled their longing for freedom, leaving the old behind and finding a new life, renewed hope, and a safe home far away from a distant, tormented, or endangered past.

I hope this array of my adventures inspires you to explore the mesmerizing history of ocean travel and helps keep the old stories alive and well, far into the future. And bear in mind, even if a mighty ship disappeared into the ocean, a part of her wreckage remains forever present, surrounded by the richness of the sea life that ornamented the broken relic. The shattered vessel serves a new, less obvious purpose, but its spirit somehow lingers on, forevermore. Ships are like people, living, breathing creatures, each with a story to tell and fascinate you with. Here are a few such stories.

Sailing Ship off Coast of Maine ~ 1876
William Edward Moran, American, 1843-1916

THE MARVELOUS SHIPS

Every ship has its own unique tale. It begins with the complex building process, where the time and place of its origin play a decisive role. The older ships from a few centuries ago, built in the 1700's, were mainly wooden. Back then, it was the *Age of Sail*, and all the building work was primarily done by hand. The entire construction process was a lengthy, tedious undertaking that involved hundreds of craftsmen and artisans, all masters of their trade. The structural material was mostly wood, except for iron bolts. The entire process followed ancient traditions and masterful artistry, and this may be one of the many reasons why older ships hold a certain magic of the faraway past.

Just think about it! Every human hand that was part of that complex and lengthy endeavor of creating the ship's every detail left an individual imprint. The carefully selected building materials were used intentionally to ensure longevity, and the hundreds of highly skilled workers who completed the extensive creative process poured their craftsmanship into the awe-inspiring creation. To this day, one may marvel at the final product of this long and demanding creative effort, which exudes so much old-world charm and uniqueness.

In the late 1800's, as the Industrial Revolution spread from Britain to other parts of Europe and North America, new building materials were introduced, and iron began to take the primary role in ship construction. This enabled the creation of much larger, more spacious vessels with ample cargo space. Steam-powered machinery increased performance, and the iron parts required less maintenance than wood.

At the end of the 19th century, British techniques were adopted in American shipyards, further advancing the industry. However, it is essential to note that sails were still used as a backup, especially on long journeys.

In the next century, through the 1900's, the materials changed yet again, this time introducing welded steel, which considerably shortened the building process and made even larger ship projects possible. The craftsmen were replaced by highly industrialized production, and the engines transitioned to using oil as fuel, taking over their coal-fueled steam engine predecessors.

No matter what time period a ship was built, it was of decisive importance to know the ship's primary purpose precisely. There are so many variables and possibilities that make each vessel truly unique. This was especially true of ships made hundreds of years ago. Their life purpose was very different: they were meant for complex missions involving long-distance ocean crossings, transporting important cargo, facilitating unpredictable journeys of discovery, and undertaking a decisive role in various battles at sea.

I have a special affinity for those old beauties because they carry the spirit of true adventure and immense human courage, uniquely shaped by that specific period of world history.

In those faraway days, the ship's captains navigated the vessels without the sophisticated instruments used today, which made each crossing or expedition a risky, extraordinarily demanding, but surely also exciting undertaking.

The passenger ships that carried countless travelers on their life-altering journeys across the great ocean exuded a mystical aura, bearing an unmistakable imprint of world history. It is estimated that between 1800 and 1930, over 50 million people permanently left the Old World, leaving Europe in search of a better life. Their final destination in America held much hope for a freer and more prosperous future, as they so desired. Undergoing such a dramatic shift while carrying new hope for their lives was also influenced by their experiences on the ship and the connections they made with other passengers onboard, which shaped the hopes and dreams and their future ahead.

These faraway, heart-wrenching departures and very long journeys were dangerous and under constant threat of mishaps on board, such as fire or disease from the crowded conditions. Much could happen while on board; but there was one possibility that carried the fiercest of dangers, and that was a shipwreck.

It is also important to mention the other kinds of ships that worked hard in war efforts or simply transported essential goods. Amongst shipwrecks were plenty of barges, flat-bottomed non-motorized vessels designed for carrying cargo. They were pushed or towed by a tugboat that could also assist in maneuvering larger ships. It is a simple fact that no vessel is too large, too small, or immune to a shipwreck; it can happen anytime, anywhere, to anyone.

There are literally hundreds of thousands of shipwrecks that occurred in the olden days, amongst them the innumerable vessels with their vulnerable and desperately hopeful passengers that forever disappeared into the ocean.

The working ships that usually carried valuable cargo had a small crew, but more often than not, they all perished at sea. They worked hard to salvage the cargo and their own lives, and showed immense courage as they fought the brutal storms at sea.

It bears mentioning that there was a certain number of sunken vessels that were recovered, and they at least partially carried forward the mission and memory of the countless people who perished at sea. Salvaging a sunken ship's remains, recovering precious personal items that rested on the seabed for hundreds of years, brings one into direct contact with the last human who interacted with the recovered treasure. It is almost as if the old memories remain intact, offering valuable insights that can be uncovered through these meaningful finds.

Even if the ship sank and unwillingly succumbed to overwhelming waves or was brought down in the conflict of an unpredictable battle, its essence somehow remained partially unbroken. Time simply stopped while the vessel rested on the seabed for centuries, sleeping in total stillness and becoming one with the ocean.

Each ship is like a living creature, a being with its own unique energy, carrying the souls through the adventures of life. During those long journeys, each passenger and crew member held on to their own set of dreams, expectations, and intentions, leaving a clear trace. A ship full of resilient and courageous hopefuls resonated differently than a pirate ship, no doubt.

During their journey, the ship's captain, crew, and all passengers merged in unison in their mutual coexistence as they faced dangerous ocean storms and often feared for their lives. The time onboard left behind a powerful memory that became a part of their individual, unique life journey.

These were the leading players in a passenger ship's life, but on a cargo ship, the overall mood was quite different. The nature of the cargo changed everything, transforming everyone on board and inspiring various events, some very predictable and others entirely beyond anyone's control. The cargo's value was a permanent tempting thought that attracted an altogether different kind of danger, as well as reckless, sometimes criminal behavior.

Of course, it was perfectly common that a passenger ship also carried gold and the riches of a few wealthy travelers on board. This also affected their general conduct, as they were aware that their entire savings and security were in constant danger of an unexpected event. The well-to-do travelers were undoubtedly nervous that something threatening or unpredictable might happen, even though they walked and behaved with a superior attitude, as if they were worth more than the rest of the less affluent passengers in tighter quarters below.

The shipmates onboard that were tending to the vessel were silently reminded that they would never have this kind of wealth in their own lifetime, but were lucky just to be near it while transporting it, and that was about it.

Of course, then came the inevitable. A wild storm, rough seas, gale winds, or perhaps a sudden attack from an enemy ship, resulting in a deadly battle. Finally, let us not exclude a sudden pirate ambush or a simple conflict of interest arising after an intended robbery of the cargo on board. All these dangerous possibilities existed and instantly changed the fate of everyone on board. If they survived the ordeal, they had a story to tell for generations to come.

But that kind of survival luck was scarce, and no matter what the cause of the shipwreck, most passengers perished, with perhaps a slight exception of a few strong men and experienced crew members. It was truly a "every man for himself" reality, and the lack of sufficient lifeboats, poor rescue organization, and speed of sinking ship in harsh weather conditions made it just about impossible to survive.

And if they didn't make it, they all sank to the bottom of the ocean along with their valuable possessions or great treasures, never to see the sunlight again. They left this world no richer than the poorest soul on board, since after all, no one takes anything with them when they depart and pass through the heavenly gates. And through the endless decades and even hundreds of years, everything seems forgotten, their lives, their dreams, possessions, and all their belongings forever lost in the great darkness of the sea.

Unless...yes, there remains a rare possibility that hundreds of years later, an expert diver like me may notice a momentary glimmer reflecting the sun above the surface of water. A hidden treasure waiting to be uncovered will call me, and I will follow the mysterious guidance of my sixth sense. I will reach down and clasp the unknown item into my hand and pull it out of eternal dankness. And in that very instant, the past meets the present and perhaps far away in another unknown dimension in the great beyond, an otherworldly sense of joy may reignite, invisibly so. The old soul will rejoice in knowing that, after all, one of their beloved items survived and regained its place in this world. Their life was lost, but a small memento remained as an afterthought.

The fascinating part of finding an old treasure or recovering an unusual, centuries-old item is the direct contact with the faraway past. I know that long ago someone held that precious item, it was so dear or valuable to them, that they took it along on their journey. These precious recovery finds reveal old stories, the fascinating details of daily lives, and offer a glimpse into a world long gone.

How was life at that time? How did people pursue their dreams, wishes, and desires? How many obstacles did they face? How difficult was it to get from one place to the other? What sacrifice was necessary, and what were their options?

All these things we may be taking for granted nowadays held entirely different sets of realistic expectations and determined the likely limitations and reachable opportunities. When I find an old silver spoon with engravings of the family crest, it feels very personal, for the spoon was a family heirloom through generations and was used for intimate rituals of meals, conversations, and daily life. Hundreds of years underwater didn't destroy it, but actually kept it in excellent condition. And after all that time, I am the one to return it to the world, to tell a story of its faraway past.

And how does that feel?
Pretty awesome, I could say, almost supernatural to an extent. The recovered object enters a new incarnation, shining once again in the sunlight and affecting everyone who sets their eyes on it. It feels as if time stood still for what seemed an eternity, but now the clock is running again. And suddenly it appears as if the faraway times may not be that far away after all. It's a game of time, the ever-restricting element of our earthly dimension. The miracle of retrieving an ancient treasure or any precious part of an old, sunken ship is quite an event.

Whenever I find a treasure in the depths of the ocean, I feel transported back to the last moment the object was afloat, above water, used, held, or carried by a human from the faraway past. I can almost sense the spirit of that person who used and eventually lost their precious item. They seem to be right there with me, and I can feel the grip of their human hand from centuries ago that held the recovered object for the very last time. How they treasured it, needed it, how important it was to them, and how dear it was to their heart. They took it on their long journey, as if sensing that this might be their unforeseen and unexpected departure from this world.

But this kind of find can only happen if the ship met an obviously fated end in a wreck. Because the truth of the matter is that, as romantic and mighty as ships may appear, they too have a limited lifetime. After a few decades at sea, they grow too old to continue due to deterioration, damage, or simply becoming obsolete and unable to compete with newer ships equipped with advanced technology. In the 1700s and 1800s, a fatal shipwreck was an almost inevitable possibility; the ship's end was not a peaceful retirement or its dismantlement for the reuse of certain valuable parts.

Each shipwreck remains underwater for what seems like eternity. It is a direct result of numerous challenging circumstances, and the question often lingers: whether the tragedy could have been prevented. I believe that most likely the destiny played its hand, and the ship's demise was unavoidable. Obviously, there were difficult circumstances, and the people on board surely did everything they could to survive. But they failed and, unfortunately, perished. And with them sank every singular item they carried on board. Together, they all disappeared into the sea, and the sunken ship lingered on the sea floor, endured the slow decay, and gave up hope of ever resurfacing again.

Until one day, a curious, courageous, and capable diver hears its quiet call and unexpectedly begins to wonder what happened to that specific ship. Or perhaps he stumbles on a find without even really looking.

This is what often happened in my experiences with treasure recovery. A thought about a specific sunken ship from long ago would suddenly enter my mind.

Perhaps someone mentioned it or called me, asking me to help them uncover the long-lost treasure at sea. Maybe I read an article, visited a museum, or followed my intuition, and often, through synchronistic circumstances, the treasure-hunting magic brought me to the destination where the lost item was resting underwater, patiently waiting for a human hand to pull it back into the sunlight.

I can tell you that finding an old treasure feels like pure magic. Everything that happened to that item suddenly opens up, offering a glimpse into its faraway past. You may feel the energy of the last human who held this object. And then there is a sense of peace, for the treasure is recovered, back from the darkness, and it enters through another doorway into a new life.

It may end up in a museum or a private collection where others can marvel at and learn about the original owner and their fascinating history, all from simply glancing at the found object. It may reveal essential details of the person who owned it, or the shipwreck itself. It may also help preserve the individual's as well as the greater historical past.

Every item you find in the recovery of an old shipwreck is precious, and I am not talking about a nominal value, or its physical appealing state. Surely a jewel, a gold bar, or a coin are valuable treasures, but so is an integral part of the ship's navigation system, a section of the mast, or a simple shoe buckle of an individual who lost their precious life. There are no human remains, but a shoe buckle may be the only thing left, so there is a historical as well as spiritual aspect to it. It reconnects us with our ancestors and opens our minds and hearts to a deeper understanding of human experience as it was in the past. One can reflect on the challenges people faced and the fragile lives that were thrown into upheaval by a fated shipwreck and an abrupt, forced departure.

As an expert diver, I can share with you that, looking at each item with careful awareness, respect, and curiosity, I genuinely appreciate my unique position to unveil these lost treasures and reclaim their essential meaning.

I have enjoyed such a privileged position for decades, and every singular find I have uncovered has been uniquely exciting. It reinvigorated my enthusiasm to find more proof of brave stories when overcoming a challenge demanded fearless courage and resilience of the human spirit. Such realizations don't evoke fear; in fact, quite the opposite. They help pry open one's heart in awe-inspiring marvel of human character and its enduring strength.

Once our physical essence perishes, what we leave behind matters to younger generations, so they can trace our footsteps and learn from our experiences. And this is what suddenly turns a shipwreck tragedy into an awe-inspiring discovery with a rare glimpse into the faraway past. It feels like some kind of time travel that is beyond exciting. The historical message captured under the sea for centuries is finally released into the ether, because in the grand scheme of things, nothing goes unnoticed and everything is seen, noted, and remembered. Brave acts of courage, therefore, remain etched in one's soul and forever live in the eternity of time.

Ship on Rough Seas ~ 1885
Max Jensen, German, 1860-1907

THE MYSTERY OF THE SEA

The aquatic realm is one of my preferred domains, and I feel perfectly at home undersea, enjoying a sense of inner peace, tranquility, and belonging. When I submerge in water, I perceive an overwhelming, deep connection with the intangible, subtle awareness, complete stillness, and absolute composure. And while every diving experience is different depending on countless factors, there is one constant sensation of weightless freedom and exhilarating sensory quietude that always brings me into a state of absolute optimal serenity. Swimming and exploring the underwater world is simply heavenly.

The first time I experienced such a magical journey was in my early childhood. It was my fortunate destiny that our family lived right on the edge of picturesque Cape Cod, Massachusetts. It was a beautiful place to grow up amidst an oasis of enchanting blue-green ponds and lakes, just perfectly tempting for an adventurous kid like me. But my love for water did not end there; in fact, when I turned sixteen, I became seriously interested in professional diving. The magic, mysterious underwater dimension mesmerized me and quickly became my favorite place to spend hours to no end.

Times were unpredictable, and at a very young age of eighteen, right out of high school, I followed in my father's footsteps and enlisted in the army. Later on, I fought in Vietnam, where I got wounded twice, but resiliently bounced back. It was a challenging chapter of my young life, as any dedicated soldier would tell you. After two Purple Hearts, a Bronze Star for Valor, and numerous recognitions for my combat distinguished service achievements, my body, mind, and spirit longed to return to the calmness of the sea. Upon my return, this desire propelled me into the world of underwater exploration. It was the optimal place to heal my senses, refine acute awareness, and help me reconnect with nature. The ease of unrestricted free movement that water offers promotes profound, deep healing and empowering positive effects on the subtle realm.

While underwater, one feels weightless and the surroundings are perfectly quiet, except for the sound of one's own breath in a most soothing and meditative way. The aquatic realm is peaceful yet filled with life and a particular kind of venerable wisdom, since the ocean itself is truly incredibly ancient. One could say, time underwater does not exist the same way it does above the surface.

It is a fascinating fact that the sheer extent of Earth's oceans and seas connects everything and everyone. When we observe the rare photographs of Earth from a faraway distance, it appears mostly blue because our planet is a spectacular world of oceans. In fact, the Pacific, Atlantic, Indian, Southern, and Antarctic Oceans form one continuous body of water that covers over 70% of the Earth's surface, which contains roughly 97% of Earth's total water.

Let's think about this for a moment and then we can reflect on the fact that our bodies are made of up to 60% of water and one thing becomes very clear; water is an essential ingredient source of all life, and our existence originates in water.

Therefore, it is no surprise that we love spending time in water. However, there are some of us who love water to such a degree that we long to "merge" with water in a deeply connected way. This is the sentiment of a true heart-centered diver.

Once you've had the otherworldly experience of spending some considerable time underwater, your perception of life above the surface changes. First, the shift occurs with smaller things and observations, like the simple fact of gravity and heaviness we experience while walking on Earth. The movement seems limited, energy-consuming, and requires much effort. You feel the restriction of the human body, and the persistent pull of Earth to keep you close.

Underwater, this changes completely, and the ease and weightlessness with which you can move is incredibly freeing and uplifting. The motion is smooth, comforting, fluid, and perfectly balanced, compared to our motion on the ground. Below the surface, you can move faster, especially if you wear fins; you feel almost like some sort of human-fish sea creature, perfectly capable of managing the different laws of gravity and weight. This affects your perception of yourself and your human limitations.

You can levitate in water above the sea floor and move swiftly headfirst. Your legs serve a different purpose; they still move you forward, but your body's headfirst position of lying in water when moving is actually less strained and feels easier. You can also turn on your back and just linger wherever you want. Water soothes and holds you like a weightless being, and this is extraordinarily comforting as well as empowering.

Swimming in itself is healing, but diving is a much deeper experience of a freer existence. Of course, there is the matter of breathing and air, but this becomes second nature, and your slower, calming breathing pattern affects your entire body, quickly placing you into an optimally tranquil state. Your mind relaxes into an existence of considerably less strain and needed effort to focus on physical movements, but instead more on your aims and goals. If you wish to move from place to place, it can be accomplished with one fluid motion.

Once you are underwater, coming back up is almost undesirable because slipping back into your heaving physical self requires effort, and you are aware of that. Of course, you have an existential good reason to come up for air, but when you're diving, that is taken care of, and there is no immediate need to come up for air. There are exceptions, of course, like when you uncover something amazing and can't wait to share it with the world and your diving partners above the surface. In such a case, you are eager to return upwards and get back into your regular human self. Even if you can share new discoveries and communicate with the team above about a fortunate find, there is nothing like seeing it in the sunlight.

After all, whatever you find was once above the surface and was meant to be here and not lost at sea for hundreds of years. There is a certain sense of inexplicable magic when an item resurfaces and becomes once again useful, even if this means recovering a portion or part of the ship that can be transformed and made into a new object. The sense of being able to participate in reclamation feels right as well as good.

Every part of the ship required a lot of work, and a part like a propeller is made of valuable materials that can be reused. Why leave it on the sea bottom in darkness, just wasting away? When you recover and bring the propeller back to the surface, it continues its life in a strange kind of way. A diver plays a decisive role in that effort. This undertaking requires very specific knowledge, abilities, and endurance. Discipline and determination play a big part in the successful recovery of a part of an older vessel that sank and has been down for a considerable length of time.

There are certainly days when you don't feel like getting into the cold water, but you must. But I can honestly say the days of fantastic diving experiences certainly outweigh those days of hesitation. After all, once you are a diving professional and treasure recovery expert, much of your existence is spent in the dimension under water. Therefore, you are forever changed and will see this regular human life above the surface as only one possible version of our existence. It is an advantageous position to be in and a true gift to be able to enjoy both worlds.

But there is one thing…in order to enjoy a diving adventure, you have to be able to let go, and I mean completely. You must trust this new world of unfamiliar sensations, because only so can you truly experience its magic. When you release your fear of the unknown, let go of attachments to this physical world and your restricted movements in it, then you can become one with water, you can merge with the ocean, and that is exceptionally freeing. Overcoming your fear of the unknown is the necessary requirement.

If you think you could not manage that, give yourself the benefit of the doubt, because remember, when you were born, you had to accept the limitations of this world and your physical body. And you obviously did it successfully, since you are here and now reading my book. Which means you can definitely learn to dive and expand your experience as a human being perfectly capable of existing in and out of water.

But that's my opinion, and as you probably know by now, I am a pretty adventurous man, and fear is not in my vocabulary. So, I do encourage you to give it a try and embark on a recreational and guided diving adventure. Your mind and perception will open up, and your heart will feel lighter, happier, and more vibrant. As a man of many seas and extraordinary deep-diving expeditions, some very challenging, but always most rewarding, I can honestly say, my love for the ocean and the mystery of the seas remains everlasting. I feel incredibly fortunate to have experienced every single deep-diving adventure that came my way.

Captain Joseph Amaral Jr. exploring the remains of Mars
Photo by Arnie Carr

Captain Joseph Amaral Jr. returning to the surface on De Braak project, Photo by Doug Ayres

BECOMING A DIVER

My journey as a serious professional commercial diver began very early on. As I mentioned, I enlisted with the army at age 18, right out of high school. I had a guarantee that I could attempt to get into special forces. They wouldn't grant me a Green Beret until I qualified from the qualification programs, which I did. I first went to infantry training and followed up with demolition training.

Next, I went to jump school and then ended up with the third special forces group. From there, I was sent to Key West, Florida, where I went through scuba school that was run by Navy SEALs.

I returned to the third group after scuba school and was shipped out to the 10th Spectrum forces group in Bastos, Germany, where I remained for a year. During my year overseas, the whole strike force team did a lot of training exercises, which entailed jumping as well as intense night operations. I was on a12-man members strike force, and the whole team came down on a levy for Vietnam. From there, I ended up with a 45-day delay in route. I ended up going to Vietnam with the 5th Special Forces Group, and that's where I remained until I was put out of the military after my second injury.

Upon my return from the army, I actually had dibs on some of the places that I could get hired, especially since I was a top-notch professional diver trained by the Navy, who successfully completed the course in the top ten.

My first job as a commercial diver was with British Petroleum in Scotland. I spent a few years there working the rigs. That was a demanding assignment that required us to live in the hyperbaric habitat complex, where we remained for days or weeks at a time. The longest time I spent in such an environment was thirty-four consecutive days. If you think this sounds like a long while, you are right.

Not seeing the sun for a month at a time is often the demand of the job in the life of a commercial diver. When you finally come to the surface, it feels like a real treat. You get a chance to get outside, walk around, breathe in the soft air, and get a real hot meal where you sit down with a bunch of the other guys and talk about the work you did at the bottom of the sea. Your body quickly adjusts, but one thing is sure: it's not a job for a claustrophobic person. It's kind of the same thing with being a paratrooper. If you're scared of heights, it's not the job you want to do.

While living in the hyperbaric habitat complex, it took a bit of time to get used to the small environment with bare basics for comfort, where we would get most of our food and equipment dry from the surface. We would do a twelve-hour shift, six hours for each diver in the water, and then we'd swap out with the other diver in the bell, and he'd go out to the bottom, do his work for six hours, and then we'd both come back to the bell that would be raised to the surface.

Next, we would go through what they call a trunk lock into the habitat and swap out with two other divers. The habitat was on the deck of a ship, so we would launch right through the bottom, which is called the moon pool. We would come up through the moon pool and hook up with the habitat and swap out. And then we would go down through the moon pool and do another twelve hours on the bottom. This was a physically very demanding job and required some serious stamina and endurance.

Eventually, I was ready to resurface and leave Scotland and came back home to Massachusetts, where I worked a few different jobs to change up my work regimen for a bit. I wanted a short break from diving, and since I was trained as an Emergency Medical Technician, I began working for an ambulance company. We were doing the rescue for the Brockton Fire Department and transported all their rescues. I quickly became tired of it and decided I felt ready to get back to diving.

An interesting opportunity arose for me to go to a school in San Diego, California, to get certified in teaching scuba diving. I was sponsored by a dive shop in a little town called Lakeville, just outside of Cape Cod. They supported me in my endeavors to become a scuba diving instructor, so I taught out of their shop for a very short time before I decided to launch my own enterprise. I didn't only want to teach scuba diving; I wanted to continue doing commercial diving as well, so I would bring in some commercial work while I still taught scuba. I truly did it all, and no job was too small or too large for me.

For a while, I had a contract with the power company, which had a new plant just outside of Plymouth, where I cleaned their net twice a week in the summer and once a month in the winter. I was quite a distance away from the reactor, so it was relatively safe. I would go into their intake, which had a very fine mesh net that went across the intake part of the waterway, and I cleaned the entire net with a strong saltwater jet, all the way across the length of the device that took the water in to cool the reactor. Needless to say, I was still doing a lot of random diving jobs at the time.

When writing about my versatile diving career, I am reminded of the tremendous knowledge I gained through the many unusual and one-of-a-kind experiences that are incredibly valuable. This is why I feel it is essential to share some of that hard-gained expertise with you, to help you understand that a commercial diver also requires an excellent understanding of complex gas mixtures. Pure Oxygen becomes toxic to the body at high pressures, leading to central nervous system effects - CNS. The symptoms can be quite severe and include visual changes, ear ringing, nausea, dizziness, and confusion. In more severe cases, it can cause a tonic-clonic seizure, followed by unconsciousness.

Many tech divers use mixed gas that they carry to the bottom. I don't believe in that. I'm not a tech diver and am old school, one could say, I go by the book. If you're going to dive deep and use mixed gas, you'd better have a chamber on the surface, ready to help you decompress from doing those deep dives, even if you're doing them on mixed gas.

I did a lot of that, especially when I was east of Scotland in the North Sea. All we used was mixed gas, either Heliox or Nitrox, and it took four guys sending a diver to the bottom to make sure that they didn't have any serious problems with making that deep dive. Divers use tanks with a mixture of gases, not pure Oxygen, to breathe at depth. The most common gas is compressed air, which contains about 21% oxygen and 79% nitrogen for recreational diving.

For deeper dives, we may use specialized mixtures like Heliox, which is Helium and Oxygen, or Nitrox, which is a blend of Nitrogen and a higher percentage of Oxygen. I, however, preferred to use surface-supplied straight compressed air, the standard, which is a mix of gases, as the air we breathe, Oxygen and Nitrogen, so I wasn't limited to the volume of gas that I was going to get.

If you don't make a decompression stop, you will suffer from a severe form of decompression sickness - DCS, often called boiling blood or the bends. If you are using straight or even mixed gas, you still have that gas trapped in your bloodstream. For commercial divers, who usually work at great depths for extended periods of time, surfacing too quickly is extremely dangerous because it can cause gas bubbles to form in the blood and tissues. So, you have to decompress and off-gass in a chamber to help you get rid of those bubbles.

In one case, when I dove on the De Braak project, I didn't make a decompression stop but came right to the surface, and my blood was boiling with the bubbles into my system. They had five minutes to get me out of my equipment and get me down to my first decompression stop, which would have been at 30 feet. Luckily, we managed on time.

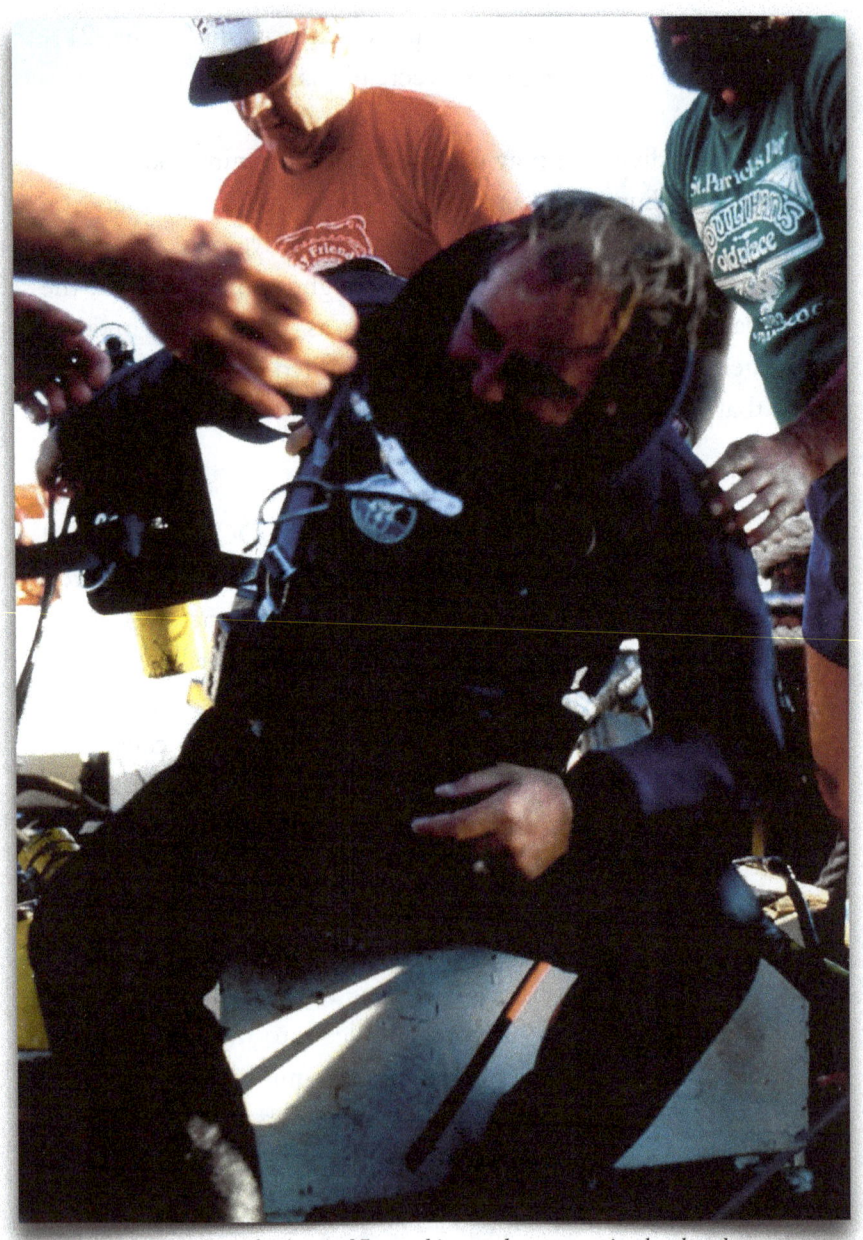

Captain Joseph Amaral Jr. rushing to decompress in the chamber, De Braak, Photo by Doug Ayres

On that project, I would usually spend a hundred minutes at 110 feet, and I decompressed for thirty minutes in the chamber where I could either sit or lie down. The decompression chamber had an inner and an outer lock. I had five minutes when I got to the surface to get down to my decompression stop. The inner lock was at my first stop at 30 feet. The simulated pressure was so that I would get in the outer lock; they slammed the door closed, and they would bring the pressure up until it equalized with the inner pressure of the inner lock. And then the door would swing open on the inner lock. I would then close it and get on what they call a decompression bin, which is coming into that system with Oxygen, so I would close the door, slam shut, and they would pull the pressure down out of the outer lock.

Next, I would decompress on the inner lock, and the duration of that process would depend on the depth and the length of the dive. For my 100 minutes on the bottom, I would need to decompress for thirty minutes in the chamber on Oxygen. It was a complex but absolutely essential procedure.

Through my lengthy professional diving career, I often specialized in specific endeavors that demanded extra knowledge and abilities. In addition to my diving expertise, I had a blasters license, so any time there was an important complex case in the shipwreck recovery project, they reached out to me for my specialized abilities. I would get involved, especially if it were a complex, hazardous undertaking. I had a demolition license so I could buy explosives, and I could utilize them most of the time offshore, where these various boats were sunk and became hazardous.

I would be called to help expertly alleviate the situation and did a lot of work for the Army Corps of Engineers.

In doing such extensive and versatile projects, I was always well informed of the new search endeavors, treasure recoveries, and interesting exploration projects that involved old shipwrecks.

My early diving adventures brought me into the close orbit of a dramatic shipwreck in Vineyard Sound, south of Nashawena Island in Massachusetts. It was the summer of 1977, and I just returned to my home near Cape Cod after getting licensed to teach scuba. And as it turned out, I was hired to instruct three scientists who worked for the Division of Marine Fisheries. They had an interesting project to study marine life in the Cape Cod Canal, where there was a power plant that took ocean water to cool its turbines and then pushed it back into the Canal. There were three scientists who had the important job of monitoring the fisheries, and while I trained them in scuba, we had a lot of fun, and they were truly great people.

It was through this assignment that I met my dear friend Arnie Carr, who was the head of research for the Division of Marine Fisheries. Through that relationship, I ended up tagging the lobsters for the same three scientists on another research project they were conducting. Arnie and I were working together, and on a hectic day, one of us forgot a set of fins, so the two of us shared a pair when we dove into the Canal, each of us wearing only one fin. It was pretty amusing, and from then on, we became great friends.

Arnie grew up on Martha's Vineyard and did a lot of wreck hunting in his life. In fact, he is quite a legendary figure in the world of treasure hunting. Considering he was always busy with professional explorations of various shipwrecks, it wasn't too long before he called me up one day with a new possible treasure hunting opportunity. He knew about a particular shipwreck and told me that if I were interested, he'd put me on the wreck as a reward for doing the diving in the Canal. Since I was eager for all adventurous explorations, I was all in. Little did I know of the complex and unsettled old debacle I would learn about when working on our project, the famed and precarious John Dwight.

But I shall begin my extraordinary stories with the most legendary wreck of them all, the formidable De Braak.

Golden Coins recovered on De Braak
Photo by Doug Ayres

MY TREASURE HUNTS

Golden Coin recovered on De Braak
Photo by Doug Ayres

The Captain's Ring from De Braak
Photo by Doug Ayres

Chapter One

THE JACKPOT

The Captain's ring on the DE BRAAK

LOCATION: Off Cape Henlopen, Delaware Bay
WATER DEPTH: approximately 90 feet
DATE OF SHIPWRECK: May 25, 1798
CAUSE: Capsized in a squall
PASSENGERS: Captain, 85 crew members: 73 officers & men, 12 Royal Marines, 9 Spanish prisoners
SURVIVORS: Maritime Pilot Andrew Allen, three Spanish prisoners, 33 crew members

One in ten million. That's right, those are the odds of finding the kind of treasure that I was lucky to uncover. It is entirely possible that one unpredictable day you'll hit the jackpot. Something profoundly fortunate could happen that will put you "on the map". The question is, will you recognize it, truly appreciate it, and make it the launchpad for other pursuits equally important that may now suddenly be within your reach?

It was in the 1980's when I was involved in the recovery of an exceptionally important treasure. One could say it was a legendary ship, since the previous thirteen failed pursuits to find its remains produced nothing. Until the fourteenth time, when I happened to be the one expert diver in the right place at the right time to uncover a beautiful and truly unique find.

But let's start at the very beginning.
The story of this extraordinary vessel began almost a quarter of a century ago in Europe, most likely the Netherlands. There were a few possibilities that the vessel might have been made in Britain or even America; however, it certainly seems that it was most likely built by Zwinjndreg in Rotterdam, sometime before the year 1781. This 18-gun brig sloop was named after the beagle, a small, quick hunting dog that often appears in old Dutch landscape paintings.

At that time, the political dynamics in Europe were very challenging since the conflict between the British and the Dutch was reignited, and thus, the fourth Anglo-Dutch war was at play. De Braak promptly began serving the Dutch army, listed as a 255-ton vessel with a single mast. The deck measured at around eighty-four feet with a fifty-seven-foot length for tonnage and a depth of hold of eleven feet. De Braak was a rather large and resilient cutter that was kept under a busy schedule as she sailed to Spain and France and remained perpetually at sea.

In February of 1793, when France declared war on the British and Dutch, followed by an invasion of the Netherlands, De Braak was ordered to assist two other warships in defense of a fortress city. The historic events that followed further complicated the overall situation, since the Dutch Prince of Orange fled into exile. De Braak was moved around for various assignments until she landed on the coast of Cornwall in England with half a dozen other Dutch warships and twenty-four merchant vessels that were used in commerce.

Because of Napoleon's unpredictable and volatile nature, an unusually violent political mood swept across the land, and suddenly, the Dutch Batavian Republic, which was under French control, entered a state of war with England. This proved most inconvenient and rather fated. In January of 1795, the British promptly stopped and prevented all Dutch vessels from leaving their ports and entered into a year-long back-and-forth negotiation, unsure about how to proceed. It dragged on and kept everyone in flux until March of 1796, when it was finally decided that all the Dutch vessels in British ports indeed now belonged to Britain. The Dutch crew members were asked to leave the ships, then the British crews took over and sailed off to Plymouth. This is where the newly captured Dutch ships were then carefully assessed for their best future use in the British Navy.

Things seemed to be going smoothly for the majority of Dutch vessels, but as it turned out, De Braak was rather unusual and required special adjustments in order to be turned into a brig, which meant they wanted to add an additional second mast. This was quite a job, and the ship was moved to dry dock, where it underwent a long list of massive changes. The overall improvements significantly upgraded the vessel, and a copper sheath was added to the hull, protecting the ship from future damage caused by barnacle growth and boring shipworms that usually presented a real threat when sailing in tropical waters. In addition, the warship was equipped with powerful carronades, a selection of fierce short cast-iron cannons which were hull-crushing and deadly in close combat, capable of smashing the enemy vessels at close range.

Once all the improvements were completed, the newly updated De Braak officially joined the Royal Navy in June of 1797. It had eighty-five officers and a brand-new person in charge, no other than the forty-six-year-old Captain James Drew. This new assignment was a long-awaited dream come true for the somewhat handsome and impulsive captain, for he played an important role in the history and ending of the famed De Braak.

His life story would not seem that unusual, were it not for the unpredictable circumstances that spun things around and caused his dramatic end. He was a British chap, born on April 19, 1751, near Cornwall in England. As the youngest of seven children, he was closest to his nearest brother, John, who was less than a year older. They were often mistaken for twins as they looked eerily alike and were simply inseparable. James looked up to his older brother and always sought his counsel. A career in the Royal Navy offered the young men the best choice to make something of their lives, since, despite being born into a genteel family as the youngest two boys, it was clear no inheritance would ever come their way.

For the first few years when James started out in his career, he was an apprentice in a variety of lower-level positions on various ships, where he gained excellent and necessary hands-on experience and important knowledge. Much to his delight, he received his lieutenant certificate at age twenty and continued to move from ship to ship, traveling for long stretches of distance and time. His brother John was more successful right from the start, which did not trigger competition or envy in James, but rather an ever-deepening sense of admiration. James wanted to make his brother proud and strived to do so his entire life.

Nevertheless, in a few years' time, he worked his way up and at age twenty-four received a good assignment abroad on HMS Preston that was set for the American colonies. Once he found himself on the western side of the globe, James's life quickly became involved in the American Revolution and all the brutality that ensued during the wars. When James Drew became entrenched in conflicts in and around Boston that was under American siege, his reputation took a turn for the worse. He somehow got pulled into the darker sphere of historical events, and in 1775, there was a rather damning report by the Americans that even reached John Adams.

The American committee informed him of James Drew's exceptional cruelty on the battlefield after the epic battle of Bunker Hill. James violent disposition towards American rebels fueled his behavior and pushed him into the darkest expression of his character, and hence earned him a bad reputation. But to allow some room for doubt, the ongoing atmosphere was indeed clouded with misinformation, and the rumors were reported by his enemies, who apparently stood by and watched James's cruel behavior without lifting a finger, so perhaps the damning reports were only partially true. The accusers themselves were of a rather dubious character, therefore much was left unconfirmed and remained speculative.

That same year, James Drew finally landed a formal commission as second lieutenant on the ship Scorpion, where he remained for the next five long years. He traveled many different routes, from New England all the way down to the southern colonies that were engulfed in the American War. Afterwards, he continued to be transferred to work on various other ships, but his career did not advance as expected. In fact, it seemed to be going in reverse. He finally became a ship commander of the vessel named Powerful in 1787, where he remained for the next two years.

Then, suddenly, James Drew was demoted with no particular reason or explanation. His career stagnated in meaningless small positions without any prominence or reward, and it appeared he was simply stuck. This was surely a disappointment for such an ambitious man, but he persisted and was finally assigned to command a smaller ship named Fly, which was traveling on various journeys between the Isle of Guernsey, Newfoundland, Canada, and Lisbon, Portugal, then finally landing back in Plymouth, England. The old and somewhat worn-out ship was in much need of repairs, so she was taken into drydock and properly tended to.

The consequence of this lengthy stay in one spot was quite predictable; since James was stuck on land for three uneventful months, after a few good weeks of rest and late-night drinking, he began longing for some human interaction. It was winter, and days were darkly gloomy while nights were long and lonely, so he got involved in a brief romantic interlude with a servant girl named Sarah, who was already promised to be married to someone else. This suited James just fine as he liked feeling like a free bird, and with his career that required long-distance travel, he had no intentions of settling down. But it sure made his waiting time easier and more entertaining. So, when his ship, Fly, was repaired and ready for sail, he was more than happy to return to sea and travel back to Newfoundland for the remainder of the year. The romantic escapade with Sarah was left far behind in the back of his memory, and he didn't give it another thought.

However, the travels eventually brought him back to Plymouth about eleven months later, at the end of the year. He conveniently remembered his last romantic pursuit in the dreary weathered British town and began entertaining the thought of finding out what his long-ago paramour, Sarah, was up to. One can only imagine the surprise when he looked her up and found her, only to receive some stunning news. She hesitantly informed him that she had borne his daughter just a month ago in the fall of 1791. She was now married, and fortunately, her new husband acknowledged the child as his own, so there would be no difficult and unfavorable situations.

Captain James was quick to step away from recognizing the child as his own and immediately chose a very different path of action. The idea of remaining in Plymouth did not thrill him at all, and waiting around the small town under the uncomfortable circumstances became an unbearable thought. Since it was a quieter time for the Royal Navy with no imminent danger in sight, it seemed he was going to be stuck in the uneasy environment with no prospects of immediate new employment. It all became overwhelmingly suffocating for James, and he made a choice that he was most familiar with and comfortable with when things got a bit out of hand.

On a whim, he just disappeared. Without any notice or forewarning, he abruptly decided to leave his naval career and reinvent a new life for himself.

How? He simply sailed off for America in pursuit of his new dreams. This was going to be a new beginning for him, and he wanted to be as far away from old, inconvenient, and unpleasant memories as possible. He landed in New York City, the most exciting, hustling, and bustling metropolis of the world, with a very different attitude from people in old England. Here, it did not matter as much where one came from as long as they spoke good English and had an entrepreneurial spirit. While in New York, James didn't sit all by his lonesome self in a corner, moping away in self-pity. Quite the opposite, he put on a new attire and got busy pursuing attractive and adventurous women of the new world. This was more interesting than anything else. He was handsome in an unusual way and certainly plenty charming, while his British accent gave him an irresistible romantic allure. Lo and behold, it did not take him long to land quite a beauty. Only four months after his arrival in New York City, he managed to sweep off her feet a most desirable and quite stunning daughter of a prominent New York businessman. He met the lovely Lydia Wattkins in the dead of winter, and they married in New York City on April 10. 1792, precisely nine days before his birthday. It was a whirlwind romance, which made James feel perfectly at home in America.

This was quite an achievement as well as a fortuitous match. The new bride, Lydia, was born on the British West Indian island of St. Christopher in the Caribbean around 1760 and was now a gorgeous creature of thirty-two, with red curly hair and pale complexion. She was about a decade younger than James, but at her age, she sensed a bit of urgency to marry and was more than happy to become a charming British Captain's wife.

But after the initial excitement and swift overdose of social events and entertainment, the marital bliss and New York lifestyle slowly became boring for the restless and impatient James, and he became rather eager to go back at sea. His adventurous spirit was hungry for more excitement, and he also felt a bit insecure about his stagnant financial position.

And to be fair, his pride and spirit were growing increasingly anxious after the new developments in the old world, when France launched a new set of conquests against all countries that stood in its way. It reflected poorly on him when he attended various fancy soirees with his wife and had nothing to answer about why he was not working for the British Navy while entirely depending on his well-to-do wife. England was not in a great state of affairs, and there was another factor that mattered to James: he needed to earn some of his own money. If he went back to England and applied for a job and made himself available to the Royal Navy, this would immediately grant him a half-salary status, which was certainly better than nothing. His pride pushed him to be a man and earn a proper living on his own.

It was exactly a year after the happy nuptials that he decided to return to Plymouth, England, and pursue new job opportunities as a captain. Lydia could not change his mind, no matter what she tried, and soon realized she could not compete with his nomadic nature and need for freedom and independence. He felt his career ambition was not over and had made up his mind. His wife, being of a practical mindset, asked him to write his last will and testament, which he did and promptly named her as his sole heir.

Then he swiftly sailed off to England, where he fiercely pursued new job possibilities. But he had no luck, no response, and simply waited for long months that slowly turned into a few years! This was a frustrating and unhappy time for James, until history turned around once more and he set off a chain of unpredictable events that created a small opening, a new opportunity for him.

It was a whole long five years later, in the spring of 1797, when Britain was in dire straits with the war against the fiercely expanding France under Napoleon's wild and far-reaching ambitions. With confident fury, he was gathering his forces along the Channel Coast, ready to attack and gobble up the tired and destitute British island.

It was precisely at that very moment that the fifty thousand Englishmen on one hundred and thirteen ships began a massive insurrection. The mutiny spread like fire all over England, and the overall situation grew rather grave. Eventually the Royal Navy agreed to the demands of the insurrectionists and managed to quickly quiet the storm, but once the mutiny was over, it broke the negotiated terms fester than imagined. It was a dark and gloomy moment in English history, and no one on the continent felt secure.

But in this stormy and dark historical cloud, Captain James finally met his long-awaited last chance and career opportunity. He was forty-six and felt this was the destined moment of good luck that had at last come his way. After years of waiting, he got a new assignment as the captain of a warship by the name of De Braak.

He was thrilled. Throughout the years, he was communicating with his beloved brother John Drew, who had a brilliant career as a very successful captain. Now at last, James had something encouraging and exciting to report to him. John was his role model, and James wanted nothing more than to make him proud. Always looking up to him, while John remained encouraging and supportive despite his younger brother's less-than-stellar career.

One specific undertaking that the older brother, John, was extremely capable of was capturing enemy ships. To him, it seemed like an effortless endeavor, and any adversary ship that came his way John immediately seized with an effortless sweeping success. This was something his younger brother James never experienced and therefore desired more than anything he could imagine. It drove him like a quiet but persistent engine, hidden from everyone else but very familiar to him and ingrained in his psyche.

It was exactly this almost obsessive ambition that was foremost on his mind when he took charge of the De Braak on June 16, 1797, with eighty-five officers and men. Only a month later, he voiced his first demand and wrote to the Admiralty requesting two mighty chase guns that were to replace two carronades. They were meant for aggressive pursuit and would make it considerably easier to get prizes in war. His petition was immediately fulfilled, and the chase guns were swiftly delivered and properly installed. Now he felt well-equipped to pursue adversaries at sea, since the British captains were instructed to bring in Spanish and enemy ships at all costs.

When he took command of the De Braak, the times were extremely turbulent, and there was a sense of urgency to get the Royal Navy ships back into the waters and far away from ports where conflict brewed further, and the seamen's discontent was overwhelming. Since it became clear the ship was going to work on long assignments in American waters, James's wife, Lydia, returned to New York, where there was a better chance they would be able to see each other whenever he came ashore.

British ships were in danger from Napoleon's French vessels, and various merchants' ships were required by law to travel in convoys with armed escorts that could offer constant protection. For that assignment, De Braak was the perfect vessel. Captain James requested that his nephew, Lieutenant John Drew, be hired as well, which was granted, and made him feel content to have a family member at his side. For the next few months, De Braak was on duty protecting the channel against Napoleon, but the persistently aggressive weather damaged numerous ships, so in December, Captain James returned with De Braak to Plymouth for some extensive repairs of a broken mast. He remained in port over the holidays and visited various family members.

But the seemingly content short pause from constant travel at sea came to an abrupt end when James received sudden, tragic news. It was January 11, 1798, when his brother,

Captain John Drew, was returning home while navigating a difficult situation at sea. As the captain of a large and powerful vessel named Cerberus, he was nearing Plymouth along with two substantial French vessels he recently captured. But because the extremely dangerous and volatile weather made it impossible to come ashore with the big ships, he decided to anchor his Cerberus and the two French captive vessels and approach the shore with a smaller barge. Fourteen men descended into the small vessel bouncing in wild waters. They tried to get near the land when a furious gust of wind escalated, and the storm became unmanageable. Before Captain John could gain control of the impossible situation, the small barge was turned over like a helpless bird in the wind and swiftly pulled into the depths of the freezing ocean waves. All souls immediately lost their lives in frigid water, except for two sailors who clung to the oars and were swept ashore. Captain John was entirely overwhelmed by the vicious waves, and his life ended within moments.

As a result of this tragedy, Captain James suffered a profound and irreparable loss. His greatest supporter, guiding light, and loyal brother was abruptly taken away. The event was a very hard blow for him since he adored and idolized his older brother, who always offered him unwavering support. This was especially tragic since Captain James was finally making his older brother proud with his own prominent position as the Captain of the De Braak. The whole family was deeply shaken, and the remainder of James's time in port was occupied with mourning and tending to family distress.

It was at that time that the unique bond between these two brothers became even more obvious when John's final will revealed that he left specific instructions. A special mourning ring was to be created and given to his younger brother, Captain James, so he could carry it wherever he went. The golden ring with personal inscription was made, and James wore it on his right-hand little finger from that day forward. Every once in a while, he would read the inscription inside the ring, and a long, heavy sigh would overwhelm his heart in grief and sadness for his missing brother.

"In memory of my brother, Capt. John Drew, drowned January 11, 1798, aged 47."

These words, inscribed on the inside rim of a wide golden ring, were supposed to help bring closure to a beloved brother's premature departure, but they never did.

In early February, only a few weeks after the tragedy, James was informed to prepare for a journey and load up De Braak with enough provisions to last six months and embark on an assignment that would take him to the Western hemisphere. A fleet of fifty vessels was to gather and travel together to America with De Braak escorting the Irish trade. After the Atlantic crossing, the large convoy would meet near Halifax, and the warships would further accompany the merchant vessels to various American ports such as Boston, New York, Philadelphia, and finally Delaware. The next leg of the journey would take the De Braak further south to escort the vessels bound for southern ports. The British were protecting the American trade as they needed American support against Napoleon, since the French considered all British ships enemies and subject to seizure.

This was not going to be an easy journey, especially considering that the American middle Atlantic seaboard was crawling with French privateers, and De Braak was the American merchant ship's protector that required to be on guard and hold an unbroken watch. After this extensive journey, De Braak was supposed to return to Halifax.

The departure was yet again delayed, since Captain James had a few concerns. His nephew, who was on board as the first lieutenant, suddenly took ill, and the captain wanted him replaced. There was also the matter of three very nasty mutinous crewmen who gave the captain concerns. He insisted and requested an immediate first lieutenant replacement, which came in the form of a friendly Irishman by the name of Thomas Hickson. The nephew left the ship and was later called to command another vessel. Little did he know that this last moment change literally saved his life.

Now De Braak was ready to depart, and on March 1, 1798, the vessel took off. On board were seventy-three officers and men, as well as twelve strong royal marines. The men were from various parts of the world, among them thirty-five British, ten Irish, as well as a man from New York, another from Hamburg, and three sailors, one from Sweden, another from Portugal, and finally, a Scott. Captain James and his crew on De Braak had to wait a few more weeks until March 14 to sail off with the large convoy that eventually gathered from various British ports. Now they were finally on their way to the Western Hemisphere.

A month later, while en route, nearing the Azores, the Portuguese archipelago in the mid-Atlantic, one of the warships noticed two strange, unidentifiable vessels and promptly sent a signal to De Braak to chase after them. It turned out to be a British ship along with a French captive vessel, so there was no immediate danger. But the weather became unexpectedly turbulent, and De Braak got further out of sight.

The forty-four merchantmen and a few escorting warships continued on their way while De Braak fell further behind. The stormy weather made it impossible for the flotilla to remain together, so they were dispersed, and while seven merchantmen were within sight, it quickly became clear that De Braak completely vanished.

For seven long weeks, no one knew where the ship was. The other vessels continued to stick together while the warships accompanied them to their destination, but there was no trace of De Braak. It simply disappeared.

There were many stories about what could have happened during that long period of seven weeks, during which no one knew the whereabouts of the De Braak. People imagined there was a raid on a Spanish fleet and a successful capture of heavily laden treasure ships. But this was mostly just wishful thinking. However, most importantly, the ship did not go down. At least not yet.

What really happened was fairly simple; the De Braak got separated from the convoy due to stormy weather and, as a result, pursued a strange sail direction that was out of sight. The ocean is a rather vast place where anything can happen. But there was some truth to the wishful guessing, since around April 30, De Braak did come upon a Spanish ship that was on its journey about two months out of Rio de la Plata in South America. The ship's name was Don Francisco Xavier, it was bound for Cadiz and happened to be loaded with 200 tons of copper, cocoa, silver, and other valuables estimated at 160k sterling.

Captain James was not going to miss this once-in-a-lifetime opportunity to finally capture an enemy ship. Despite Xavier's large size and very capable captain, De Braak gave it all she got and managed to quickly startle and occupy the Spanish ship. Next, under directive from Captain James, a prize crew, which was a small detachment group of sailors from De Braak, led by Lieutenant Thomas Griffith, took control of the captured Xavier. Eleven sailors were placed on board the captured ship to help sail it to a friendly port, while guarding the enemy crew, who were sent below deck. The Spanish captain and officers were chained to the cannons, so they could not rebel or repossess the vessel.

An English Man-of-War Taking Possession of a Ship 1783, Robert Cleverly, English, 1747 - 1809

The prize crew's primary tasks were to prevent any recapture attempts and ensure the ship was ready for a prize court to adjudicate its fate once they all came ashore. Fifteen Spanish seamen were taken prisoners. Captain James was elated and bursting with self-confidence, despite a small part of him feeling a deep regret that his brother John was never going to hear about this latest grand achievement. He wanted to make John proud since he finally accomplished something, but his brother was already gone. Little did he know that his own glory was short and passing, for this was to be his first and last prize ship. He was ready and eager to head for Delaware and hopefully rejoin the convoy.

On May 25, 1798, an American sloop, the President, suddenly saw the De Braak off Cape Henlopen, mistook it for an enemy, and fired a few shots, but fortunately, De Braak successfully escaped. By afternoon, De Braak and her captive vessel Xavier were finally prepared to enter Delaware. As was usually the habit, a maritime pilot was supposed to help navigate the vessel into the harbor so they could resupply. The harbor pilot, Andrew Allen, came on board and began steering the ship out of dangerously unpredictable waters so they could safely enter the harbor.

But after such a long and arduous journey, Captain James' patience was wearing thin, and the idea of someone else commanding his ship simply agitated him. He just wanted to bring the vessel ashore, resupply, and then sail home so he would finally have some personal time to reunite with his wife, Lydia, who was waiting for him in New York. His irritated disposition and need for control seemed obvious, and he was in no mood to consider the maritime pilot's suggestions, but instead he expressed a wish they should celebrate the fortuitous return and capture of a great prize ship, Xavier, that lingered close by. He went downstairs into his elaborate captain's quarters to get a drink and have toast with the harbor pilot. Truth be told, Captain James had been enjoying a few evening drinks the entire journey, for it helped him soothe his grief, mellow his nerves, and feel more courageous than his slightly bruised sense of self-confidence.

Meanwhile, the pilot Andrew noticed fast approaching dark clouds causing sudden spurts of vicious wind and quickly ordered the light sails screwed up. The crew obeyed and began preparing for a possible storm. Upon Captain James's return on deck, the pilot quickly informed him of the situation and his given command, which angered the captain and triggered his impatient and unreasonably controlling nature. He did not hide his displeasure and promptly reversed the command, angrily ordering the crew to sheet the sails once again so they could sail ashore. He also didn't waste any time to confront the pilot Andrew and utter his last famous words:

"You look out for the bottom, and I'll look out for the spars!"

This impulsive command was a crucial and careless mistake. The harbor pilot was well versed in navigating stormy waters, and this process required his command of the entire vessel, not just "the bottom," to avoid a possible dangerous rock. But Captain James did not think of that, for all he saw was his unwavering power over the ship, the captured prize vessel, as well as all the seamen involved.

Shortly thereafter, De Braak entered Old Kiln Road, and everyone onboard was excited to land since they were only a mile away from Cape Henlopen Light. Captain James decided to come ashore in a six-oared cutter, which was a smaller vessel, and quickly replenish his fresh water supply. The captured Spanish ship Xavier lingered closely with the remaining nine-man prize crew and likewise planned to follow and stop for fresh water. Everyone was ready to let the captain and crew ashore.

But before anyone set foot onto the smaller barges, everything changed in an unpredictable, sudden upheaval. It all happened so unexpectedly and out of nowhere that all they heard was a frightfully violent thunderous roar, closely followed by an inexplicably powerful gusty whirlwind. It struck De Braak and fiercely pulled it into a deadly swirl that overtook the entire vessel. In a shocking scene, the ship's brig heeled over on her beam ends with such a rapid and unpredictable force that it caused the hull to fill up with unfathomable speed while the water poured in through the open hatches. Since the weather had been clear up until now, the deck openings were not closed, and once the ship capsized, the lower levels were flooded in an instant. Crashing waves hit over, enveloping the vessel, and everyone below the deck was instantly doomed, while topside, the heavy artillery broke and flew across the deck, killing everyone in its way. It was a brutal ordeal tossing De Braak like a tiny, fragile matchbox swallowed by the angry sea.

Thirty-three of the most resilient men struggled to scramble aboard the cutter that was alongside and saved themselves onto the captured Spanish ship Xavier. De Braak sank rapidly, with the forty-seven men instantaneously gone. At the end of the sudden, violent ordeal, De Braak was submerged, but somewhat straightened up, and all that was left was the masthead, eerily standing above water. Of the captured Spaniards, only three survived when they clung to a floating mahogany-oak captain's sea chest and somehow made it ashore. It is quite possible they were the ones who ignited and spread the rumor about De Braak carrying massive treasures of jewels, gold, silver, and diamonds from Peru, Mexico, and Spain. These were the rumors that lingered and tempted treasure hunters for many decades after the shipwreck.

And just like that, in a matter of minutes, the unfortunate Captain James was simply gone, swallowed by the sea. His dreams and desires for a victorious return with a captive ship were sunk and lost along with everyone else's lives. The maritime pilot Andrew Allen closely witnessed this unspeakable tragedy in utter horror but somehow found the courage to throw himself onto the little cutter alongside the sinking De Braak. It was sheer good fortune that he landed in one piece, despite breaking his leg. Nevertheless, he did save his own life.

It was a disaster that left everyone shaken to the core. Later on, several crew members went up the Delaware River to inform the British consul of the tragic and catastrophic outcome. The loss was substantial.

In the odd twist of fate, the captured Spanish vessel Xavier came out unscathed and continued to sail with the small prize crew from De Braak all the way to Philadelphia, where it was taken under control by the English. Captain James gave a prior order in case the two ships were to separate, that the Spaniard vessel should go on to Philadelphia. Little did he know at the time that Xavier would make it, while his own vessel would dramatically sink and take his very own life with it. He perished precisely 134 days after his beloved brother, Captain John Drew, under eerily similar circumstances.

Barely three days later, Captain James's body washed ashore and was found near the Cape Henlopen Lighthouse. A black employee by the name of Jacob Bailey found the remains washed ashore and reported them to the authorities.

When the news was delivered to Captain's widow, Lydia, who waited for him in vain, she was beyond devastated in realizing her husband was never to return. She mourned his loss alongside the Drew family, who later erected an elegant marble plaque in St. Nicholas Church in Saltash, England. It included all three of their family seamen who lost their lives: brothers Captain James and Captain John, as well as their nephew First Lieutenant James William Drew, all departing within a short space of one year's time.

James's beautiful wife, Lydia, remarried two years later and lived in a palatial home with her wealthy new husband. On occasion, they were driven about in a chariot, but despite her comfortable life, she never forgot her beloved first husband, James, and erected a memoir to mark his grave in the churchyard of St. Peter's in Lewes, Delaware. The only surviving direct relative of Captain James Drew was his illegitimate daughter Maria, who lived in England and never saw her real father. To her, he remained an eternally unsolved mystery.

The very first attempt to salvage the De Braak occurred quite quickly, in fact, a few months after the shipwreck, in August of the same year. But the mission was repeatedly delayed for various reasons. Another ship sank soon thereafter and occupied everyone's time, and when they finally arrived at the scene of the De Braak shipwreck in late summer, they quickly determined that the vessel was so violently shaken, it was most likely filled with mud and sand, and it would not prove worthwhile to go through the expense of the salvage efforts. But the British consul at Philadelphia, by the name of Phineas Bond, persisted. He made a complex plan and intended to gather four ships and jointly attempt the salvage. However, the ship's crew members felt rather unhappy about the small payment offered, which depended on the resulting recovery of the salvage.

Oddly enough, this kind of predestined, delayed, and complicated predicament followed the De Braak her entire sunken life. The British planned to salvage and then move the ship to Philadelphia, where they could properly repair it. But then, suddenly, there was an outbreak of yellow fever, which made matters even more challenging. The British consul's explicit instructions were to pay attention to many valuables on board, which ignited and further fueled the rumors that the ship carried great treasures. But in fact, the consul was talking about the ship's valuable equipment and not coffers of jewelry and cases of gold.

Finally, the recovery effort was made where they used cables and hooked the main mast in attempt to lift and pull the ship into more shallow waters where they could salvage it, but it was utterly impossible, and all they ended up doing is to break and carry off the main mast, while the hull remained in place, so after three failed attempts they simply gave up. The copper and silver cargo on Xavier made up for the financial loss of De Braak, but there were no treasures or gold on the Spanish vessel, and even if there had been, Captain James would have had it promptly transferred to De Braak, which the crew would have certainly witnessed. But this did not happen.

The Xavier was sold, and the sailors eventually received the prize money, as it was often the only payment for seamen over and above their wages. They got some change, but the biggest portion always went to the captain and admiral. As with everything else connected with De Braak, even the payout took forever, with the very last payment disbursed twenty-four years later in 1822, when the last widow of De Braak's boatswain finally received the monies due. This chapter of De Braak's story was finally closed, and for almost two hundred years, no man would get their hands on the sunken vessel. The main reason was fairly simple, because of the failed first attempt that tore off the mast and the mizzenmast and thus disassembled the two pieces of the ship, the somewhat visible mast was in the wrong location, separated from the hull that remained a considerable distance away. Everyone who searched for the sunken ship looked in the wrong place since the location of the vessel's body was lost. De Braak's remains were in deep waters and did not present a hazard to other ships, and since they were never found, they remained partially intact and were never blasted with dynamite, but slept undisturbed for decades.

Captain Joseph Amaral Jr. with Harvey Harrington and the Captain's Ring from De Braak, Photo by Arnie Car

After thirteen failed recovery attempts that took place over the next hundred and eighty-six years, the gods finally smiled upon De Braak and graced her with a partial return to glory. And this is when a set of destined circumstances knocked on my door and called me to the mysterious place where the mighty ship slept her deep and forgotten sleep at the bottom of the ocean.

This fascinating story began in 1984 when I was offshore with my boat called the Sonoma that I used for charters. One unexpected day, I got a phone call from my friend John Fish, who was trying to get in touch with me because he wanted me to go with him to Delaware. He was hired as a historian by our mutual friend Harvey Harrington, who was leading a potentially interesting project.

He asked John to look at a particular shipwreck and see if he could determine whether or not it was the one he was actually looking for. It was all shrouded in mystery, and John didn't want to go by himself, so he asked me if I'd go, and I said, indeed, I would love to go. So, we left and drove up in my truck a couple of days later and got to Lewis, Delaware. We went out into the ocean the very next day on a slack tide, which is a brief period when the tidal current is weakest, and the water is calm, which makes it a safer and easier time for diving.

We were on a small steel-built, very low-profile fishing boat that Harvey had hired, called the Seneca, with Donnie Evans as the captain. So, in the very beginning of this big adventure, it was just John Fish, Harvey Harrington, Captain Donnie Evans, and me.

When we began to dive and explore this mysterious wreck, I first remained on the sunken ship's deck, where there was very low visibility. Since the site was close to the harbor in Lewis, Delaware, the tidal influx of the rising tide, which brought seawater into the bay, obviously influenced the diving. On an outgoing tide, we had very little visibility, and on an incoming high tide, the visibility was at its best. This is why we dove at slack tide since there was a lot of current in that particular location. We planned our diving around the tides, so we'd have calm water.

After the first dive, I said to John,
"We were just on the deck. Did you see all those cannons?"
And he replied,

"Don't say that. Don't say that. You don't know how many times I've thought I was looking at a cannon, and we lifted it up, and then it turned out it wasn't a cannon at all."

I repeated,
"John, read my lips. Those are cannons."

We kind of got over that hesitant part and were doing two dives a day, measuring the ship's remains while I was photographing. And we were trying to determine whether or not the information we were gathering matched what we thought to be De Braak. This was, of course, the preliminary research, since Harvey had to get two separate permits, one to search and the other to salvage, because we were in the state's territorial waters. While he was trying to determine whether this was De Braak, he remained on board for the first five or six days that we dove and made a video.

Next, he got the search permit, and then we determined that we were going to lift the cannon so we could finally find out and confirm whether it was De Braak. John had access to somebody who could send him the serial numbers on the cannons, so this made perfect sense.

We began by lifting one of the long guns, which was a twelve-pounder, and brought it to the surface. And, of course, because it was made of iron, it was all encrusted, which made it hard to tell what it was. We had an A-frame on the stern of the Seneca, which was a fishing workboat. I rigged it, and our Captain Donnie Evans was able to lift it right up on board.

And we thought, yeah, this must be it! We were quickly able to uncover the King's broad arrow, which was a symbol of royal ownership. Anything that was made by the crown always had the King's broad arrow inscribed on it. We even found long brass nails that had the broad arrow carved into them. But here it was, a clear proof with the broad arrow as well as a crown on the cannon, poured right into the foundation.

Now, we were in a bit of a predicament since Harvey had a search permit, which he could lose if anybody from the state found out that we had actually lifted or taken anything from this wreck. What he needed next was a salvage permit, so we had to temporarily place the cannon in a river when we went by on the way back into Lewis, where Captain Donnie used to keep his boat.

After the cannon helped us confirm we had De Braak, Harvey applied for a salvage permit, got properly assigned, and then we had to rig up the cannon to pick it up again so we could salvage it. He was the one who jumped in the water to get it done, since I told him that I was not getting in that water with snakes. It was pretty funny, but he stoically got into the river and rigged up the cannon despite the eels all around him.

John and I continued to make two dives a day on scuba on a slack tide, usually about thirty minutes on a single tank, measuring various things. During the high tide, I had some decent visibility and was coming down one side of the vessel that I hadn't spent a lot of time on, and suddenly found something sticking out of the bottom that looked like coins. And it turned out to be a concretion of over 200 coins and two gold coins mixed up in the middle! It was quite a find, and everyone was beyond thrilled. This was getting very exciting, and we all felt as if we were on the brink of something somewhat monumental.

Harvey eventually secured the first major vessel that we used during the first year. It was called the Mariner and was about 86 feet long, open at the stern, and had accommodations, which were very convenient. It had a forward raised pilot house to provide better visibility, and we put a two-man double lock decompression chamber on it, and that was that. It was a pretty old system. Terry Edgecombe was the gentleman that Harvey hired to run the dive operations, and he had a trailer with his SAT – saturation diving system and state-of-the-art devices on board with a dive system that handled all the air or different gases that divers used.

In addition, we had a whole trailer that held a communication system because we were mixing gas for the diver's habitat and for the bell that was transporting the divers to and from the sea floor. The air supply hose was tied to the diver and was able to measure his ongoing depth, so he was tended to during the descent into the water and during the entire stay underwater. And when the diver came up, depending on the amount of time that he spent at depth, the Navy dive tables determined how much time he needed to spend in the chamber. And we'd switch off from breathing air and go into oxygen after thirty feet. So, the triage system was placed on board the Mariner, and we made some anchors to hold the trailer, because it was a steel vessel.

The system was set up inside the trailer, and we welded the chamber to the deck as well, so it remained a permanent fixture on the Mariner, and we used it for the whole first season.

Our dives were around 110 feet, and a bit less on the low tide flow. There was an approximately six or seven-foot tidal change in that location, so it was already around 100 feet when we were on scuba, which wasn't a big deal. We had fifty minutes that we could safely spend underwater without getting into a decompression. We weren't down there that long, and in the first week, all we did was inspect the hull and do some measurements, while trying to figure out the layout of the wreck. The team used the side scan sonar equipment, which emitted a fan-shaped sound pulse to the left and right of our moving vessel. It created a detailed image of the seafloor by interpreting the strength of the returning echoes. A two-dimensional image of the seabed was created, with harder objects appearing darker and softer areas or shadows appearing lighter, which helped produce a detailed chart of the sea floor. We were also using blowers to dislodge sand as well as the airlift, a giant vacuum cleaner that removes layers of sediment while we searched for treasures.

Right when we first started the salvage, I was incredibly fortunate and immediately uncovered gold coins everywhere. It was beyond exhilarating and made me feel like I was in seventh heaven. A treasured find is what every diver dreams about, and since this is a very challenging profession, a significant reward like that feels truly special. It is pure luck, magnified by an inner knowing that you were the fortunate one to recover an old historic object that waited for your hand's touch for many, many years. Sometimes centuries.

The next exciting find was a majestic silver chalice, sitting on the sea floor, just waiting to be picked up and brought back into the light. I remember my heart pounding as I pulled it from the sand and held it in my hands. What a gorgeous object!

And then our search effort took a most decisive turn in the entire De Braak journey of discovery. I detected the magnificent captain's quarters and was the first man to set foot onto that untouched world of the faraway past. I immediately understood the significance of that meaningful historic space and was able to salvage quite a bit of the captain's personal effects, or his taken treasures, right from his quarters.

Among other items, I found a crystal glass-covered locket, containing a lock of hair which was most likely from his beloved brother who died just a few months before Captain James. This was considered a popular mourning jewelry in 1700's England. When I held the crystal locket in my hand, it opened my eyes to the touching realization that a grown, brave man was in deep mourning for his beloved brother. It felt very emotional and tender at the same time.

Since the ship sank hard, everything was kind of settled to the starboard side, and there wasn't any furniture left. All that remained was the hull, the beams, and the timbers that held it together. There was also a significant amount of copper because De Braak was a well-put-together government vessel.

The whole bottom had an exterior copper sheet to protect the hull from the worms. It was still in the hull, but all along the starboard side, where it had lain over at the very stern part of the vessel. The whole upper part of the cabin had windows, so there were many glass panels, because in the ships from the 1700s, they always liked to let a lot of light into the captain's quarters.

I also found a great number of candle holders and could easily imagine the captain sitting in his cabin rooms which were the best quarters on the vessel. This is where he was late at night, writing into his journal by the candlelight, with the powerful sound of ocean waves swaying De Braak and carrying her across the vast distances. I uncovered something else that I felt was significant: two dueling Derringer guns that the captain probably wore in his sash, because they were a matching set. There were some round balls, and nearby, I also found the captain's beautiful sword. The treasures just kept coming, and the very next thing I detected was a fine watch that was encrusted with Captain Drew's family crest, featuring a roaring bull with three sheaves of wheat in his mouth.

These significant, well-preserved discoveries in the captain's quarters came upon me unexpectedly but certainly caused a very profound emotional experience, for I felt like I was visiting his sacred space where he lived, slept, reflected, made decisions, and dreamt of his future. He also grieved for his brother and longed for his wife, so the space was permeated with a certain unspeakably, deeply touching sentiment, almost like unexpressed poignant feelings trapped in the infinity of the faraway past.

And then something happened that changed the course of my life. Lying on the sea floor, gleaming in the sand, was a perfectly flawless golden ring, just as it came from the mint. What could be more difficult to find at the bottom of the ocean than an almost two-hundred-year-old captain's ring? It is clear there is no way to plan or even predict such a find, it is simply pure, sheer, crazy good fortune. But like all good karma, you must earn it, and it sure looks like I earned the right to be the lucky man to find this unique one-of-a-kind treasure, and I remain eternally grateful.

Of course, at the time, I had no idea how significant it was. Since I found so many stunning artifacts and was genuinely overwhelmed by the volume of treasures, I simply picked up the ring and stuck it in my diving glove, so I wouldn't lose it. It was so small it wouldn't even fit on my little finger. And in the same area where I uncovered the ring, I also found all kinds of gold coins. There were more than thirty golden coins in that one little area where I found the ring, and I was honestly more interested in the gold coins than in this little ring. It was one of the last things I found before my time was up, and I had to return and come up after my 100 minutes on the bottom.

I had only a few short minutes to quickly get into a chamber, or the gas in my bloodstream was going to come out in little bubbles, and I could get the bends. It was very close, so the team was anxious to get me to my first stop as soon as possible. I was finally inside, breathing oxygen out of a BIBS mask that had a built-in breathing system. And suddenly, I heard the chamber operator coming over to the comm system in the chamber.

And he read me the memorial inscription on the inside of this little ring:

"In memory of my brother, Capt. John Drew, drowned 11 January 1798, aged 47."

And I just couldn't believe it. I said, "I never saw that," while everyone on the other end was clapping, hugging, jumping up and down, and screaming from utter joy. You know, of course, I never saw the inscription, simply because I never looked. While I was underwater, I found the ring, shoved it into my glove, and I thought that was that. Now the significance of what I found really started to hit home.

This ring was exceptionally important because its unique inscription instantly and irrevocably confirmed who the ring belonged to. And consequently, it was an unequivocal proof that the uncovered ship was no other than the legendary De Braak.

This is when Harvey made the second public announcement that we found De Braak. The first press conference occurred a few months ago when we began our search and found the canon. At that time, we went out there on the ship with a TV camera and crew on board and a reporter from NBC. It was rather funny, since they had me right on the stern of the vessel with this immense, beautiful treasure. It was a citron porcelain water container that was used for drinking water. They wanted me to lift that for the news footage, and the only thought in my mind while I was bringing it up was, "Suppose I lift this up and it hits the back of the boat and shatters on national TV!"

I rigged it up with a small lift bag, and they were able to get the shot on board the Seneca. It was a big feature on the news that night about us lifting this citron porcelain water container, and incidentally, this was the first time I photographed the gudgeon and a pendle. The gudgeon is the after part of the ship that attaches a rudder and holds the rudder in two positions. Funny enough, I have a photograph of the gudgeon with a lobster living under it, which I find very entertaining. It goes without saying that it was remarkably helpful that De Braak was as intact as possible under the circumstances.

Now, a few months after the first press conference, things progressed in a dramatically positive way. Since we uncovered the massive treasure load in the captain's quarters and I found Captain James Drew's memorial ring with an inscription, it all suddenly became quite a big deal. This press conference was a major news event and included reporters from at least four different broadcasting companies: ABC, CBS, and NBC.

All six divers from the first year were there, and Arnie and I sat close together. Since I was the person who found the ring, it immediately propelled me into the public eye, and I suddenly found myself on the CBS Good Morning show and in Time magazine. At this big press release event, we all wore the same kind of polo shirt with the De Braak name on it and a picture of a coin. John Fish's wife designed and made the shirts, so we all looked like part of a team. Each one of us was properly introduced, and our press manager, Stacy Wolf, gave this big presentation of how professional we were and how great the project was. Harvey was thrilled and showed a big container of gold coins, and of course, the captain's ring was a big hit.

The interviews aired round the clock for a couple of days in four states: New York, Delaware, Maryland, and Pennsylvania, and everything was quite a big deal.

As a result, public curiosity became insatiable, and the whole time we were working that summer, there were always people coming from various publications eager to write an article and see it in action. It was like an exciting adventure, a treasure hunt, the world was eager to see and participate in. We even had some broadcasters from overseas who wanted to be with us out on the vessel while we were working. They were eager to be as close as possible to the daily treasure recovery events, always enthusiastic in anticipation of what would emerge from the ocean.

Being a commercial diver is working in a kind of abstract world where you're dealing with the client and whatever you're supposed to be doing on the seafloor. Very rarely do you see the kind of publicity that we were receiving for working on this wreck. It was, shall I say, all very unusual and truly an extraordinary experience.

Our work continued, and we uncovered more interesting finds, such as an awful lot of rum bottles with a GR on them. And we were thinking, GR? Was that George Rex's? John found out later that they used the symbol from the tavern that they got the rum from. That symbol was on their bottles, and a lot of the rum bottles that we recovered still had the cork in them. We also found beautiful porcelain, where they stored their rum, pears, peaches, or whatever they served. We found a ton of fascinating objects that revealed much historical information.

The team rented a facility, used it as a laboratory, and placed all the recovery into conservation labs. Robert Reed was an excellent archaeologist who was hired by the state to oversee all our salvage efforts. The collection of finds grew every day and included all the ship's cannons, a lovely assortment of china from the officer's table, a long-barreled pistol, a scabbard, hundreds of buckles, toothbrushes without bristles, pulleys from the rigging, a bootjack, a scrub brush, and a pewter spoon, engraved with the nickname Mitch.

And then there was the De Braak bell. When I rigged the bell, and we lifted it onto the vessel, we were fully expecting to see the name De Braak. But to our surprise, it didn't have that name, and instead, the letters said La Patricelle. It became clear that when they were refurbishing De Braak during one of its new incarnations or ownership shifts, they actually took the bell off another ship and put it on De Braak.

There were many adventures and interesting experiences that occurred during our long search. Once, while we were working the wreck, we were in a three-point war. We were on board with our Mariner, and a large ship from Copenhagen got caught and unfortunately parted off one of our wires. We had one of our divers in the water, and the ship swung on the anchors that we had out and almost ran down our vessel. It ran right down one side of us, and John Reedy was running down below, grabbing life jackets and bringing them up and throwing them at the guys, because everyone thought they were going to capsize our ship, the Mariner. They were that close you could look up and see them right there.

The Copenhagen ship went to pick up a harbor pilot, and it was he at the helm who almost ran us down. Donnie Chalker was our diver who was on the bottom at that time, and we dragged him right across the wreck. The tide was running, and the boat swung on our mooring wires and pulled Donnie right across and off the wreck, so he landed in the mud. After the vessel went by him, we were able to secure him, get him back up on board the deck, and get him in the chamber. He did his decompression while we were hanging on two wires, and it wasn't until the next morning that we went out with Donnie Evans to reset our anchors. And that's how we worked, we moored - secured the salvage vessel right over the De Braak wreck. And we would work from the port side, and the diver would get lowered down right onto the vessel and move to a place on the record that he had to work. We did it by grids made from PVC, and we had to drill holes in them to prevent sinking.

During the first year, the six divers worked only during the day and never at night. In the second year, we ended up with a bigger vessel that was ninety feet long, and we began with two ships that had twelve divers in the crew. I worked on De Braak for three seasons, which meant three summers, and by the month of November, we were done. I was usually one of the last divers to leave. Arnie took his vacation from the Division of Marine Fisheries for about a month for two seasons, and we got really close during our time working together. He was incredibly supportive, kind, and treated me almost like his son.

One time, Arnie and I were both put in the water at the same time. And the way it was set up, they could talk to one diver at a time while he was on the bottom, but they couldn't speak to both of them at the same time. I was moving and picking up a lot of loose material and putting it into a big clam basket, and somehow, I must have knocked out the communication wires with the surface, because they lost communication with me. They still had it with Arnie, but they didn't have it with me. This was, of course, concerning. There was another guy on board who was in the communication shack listening to what was going on, and apparently, he got all hyper because he couldn't contact me, and I wasn't responding. The rack operator, Terry Edgecombe, immediately notified Arnie to go find me and see what was going on with me. And there I was, working and humming to myself, since I used to constantly sing to myself underwater, which would make the technical guys crazy.

They'd be saying, "Amaral, shut up!" That's what I would get.

"We're trying to listen to what you're doing; we don't want to listen to you sing."

And I'd say, "Okay, okay." It was all very funny.

In a few minutes, Arnie found me, came up close, and gently whacked me on the side of the helmet while fiddling around with the connection to the comms system, and it finally came back. Now the rack operator had communication with both of us, and all was well. Afterwards, it was one of the only times that Arnie and I ever got in that double lock decompression chamber together, since they had to bring us up together, and we still had to do our stops in the chamber.

Once we got in the chamber, Arnie began kidding around, saying, "You know, no matter what you do, Amo, you screw up. How the heck did you manage to knock off your comm wire?"

I laughed, "What do I know? I probably knocked it off. You hit me in the head underwater!"

We all had a great laugh about it and remembered this event as a good joke for years after. Some of the best times of my life have been underwater. I just loved exploring the magical dimension below the surface and feeling total inner peace as I listened to myself breathe. It was always one of the most relaxing experiences for me. I belong in the underwater world as well, that is for sure.

The recovery mission shifted after I left the project, as did the management team, and an intense debate ensued about how to proceed. Eventually, the next project management decided to lift the De Braak hull out of the water, an unwise decision that damaged the delicate archaeological site and sparked considerable discussion among the salvage, diving, and historical preservation communities. Consequently, a new protective law, the Abandoned Shipwreck Act of 1987, was signed by President Ronald Reagan. The act directs guidelines for underwater parks, asserts the US title to shipwrecks on state lands, and states the US owns shipwrecks on public lands. This helps prevent improper handling of any shipwreck remains.

The De Braak story and the recovery of its treasure, especially Captain James Drew's golden ring with a personal inscription, surely touched everyone's heart. The unusual bond and love between two brothers remain a beautifully inspiring reminder of what matters most in life.

Even though Captain James Drew never achieved the level of success and recognition as his older brother, Captain John, in the halls of history, it is James who is better known.

Why? Because of his brother's memorial inscription in the ring that was found a few hundred years after both men perished. The brothers remain eternally connected beyond time and space, and I feel almost certain that their souls are content with how history remembers them.

They chose the same career path and left this world under eerily similar circumstances, yet remain linked by a loving inscription in a ring that binds them together forever. Life and death are but a passing illusion in this cosmic puzzle. What really matters is the love that endures until the end of time.

Golden coins from the De Braak,
Photo by Doug Ayres

The Mariner salvage vessel, first year of search for De Braak, Photo by Doug Ayres

Diver run's drive operations from the rack, Peterson operator, De Braak, Photo by Captain Joseph Amaral Jr.

The Mariner salvage vessel, dive shack, two-man decamp on stern, De Braak, Photo by Captain Joseph Amaral Jr.

The dive crew on De Braak, Left to right upper row: Harvey Harrington, Jim Cummings, Captain Joseph Amaral Jr., Tom Harding, Jeff, Front row: Arnie Carr, Jack and Obe O'brian
Photo by John Fish

The recovered bell from De Braak,
Photo by Doug Ayres

*The recovered golden chalice from the De Braak,
Photo by Doug Ayres*

Captain Joseph Amaral Jr. with golden chalice from the De Braak, Photo by John Fish

*Recovered golden coins from the De Braak,
Photo by Doug Ayres*

*Recovered utensils & coins from the De Braak,
Photo by Doug Ayres*

A glass vase recovered from the De Braak, Photo by Doug Ayres

Ceramic vases and cups recovered from the De Braak, Photo by Doug Ayres

Steamer "St. Lawrence" 1850, similar to John Dwight
Artist James Bard

Chapter Two

THE GANGSTER

The Unsolved Murder on John Dwight

LOCATION: *Vineyard Sound, south of Nashawena Island, MA*
COORDINATES: *41-23-26N / 70-52-36W*
WATER DEPTH: *85'*
DATE SUNK: *April 6, 1923*
CAUSE: *scuttled – intentionally sunk*
PASSENGERS: *About twelve souls on board, all crew members*
SURVIVORS: *Eight perished, others survived and disappeared*

The John Dwight shipwreck was a very unusual case. To this day, it remains marked by a puzzling and unresolved demise that indicated a rather haunting end. In fact, the whole story reads like a perplexing crime novel with plenty of dark, shady characters and clandestine behavior, all happening on the foggy coastline of the mystical Nashawena Island region, known for its treacherous waters and perilous maritime past.

The John Dwight was a steamboat built in 1896 at Thompkins Cove, New York, by the Rodeman Company. The small town did have a notable history in vessel construction, especially of smaller crafts, but was mostly busy with the local limestone quarry. Nevertheless, this particular ship was constructed there and had a coal-fired boiler, a 250-horsepower steam engine, and one propeller. It was made of wood, with one mast and one derrick, which is a handy lifting device used to hoist cargo in and out of a vessel. At a 127 feet length, 27 feet width, and 8 feet of depth in proportions, it was a noteworthy vessel and a strong, solid, and hardy worker. The tonnage capacity was 151, so she could carry some substantial cargo at a speed of 10 knots or 12 mph.

The vessel was owned by George T. Moon and was first used in the Menhaden Atlantic coast fisheries as a freighter. After two years of transporting catches, fuel, supplies, and taking fish back to port, her destiny dramatically changed. On May 6, 1898, it was purchased by the US Navy. It was a precarious time during the Spanish – American War, and the vessel was named USS Pawnee YT-21. It was assigned to the 3rd Naval District, and its primary role was operating as a harbor tug, towing, and assisting larger naval vessels at the New York Navy Yard in Brooklyn. The ship continued its quiet service as a harbor tug for many years after the war and even suffered a minor collision in April of 1910, with the steamer Bloomsburg off the New York Navy Yard, but thankfully, the incident did not result in any damage to either vessel. Clearly, she was of the strong and resilient kind.

The ship was finally decommissioned on March 24, 1922, and sold only a few months later in July of 1922. She was operating again for commercial use, so her name was restored to her original title as the John Dwight. The man who purchased the elder ship was a sixty-year-old Captain Lewis N. Blix of New York, a well-known yacht racing expert who was involved in marine salvage work. Apparently, the area experienced severe coal shortage during the previous winter of 1922, so Captain Blix was hard at work salvaging coal for the following winter, and he was excellent at it. Under his ownership, the John Dwight vessel became a part of the captain's successful shipwreck recovery effort, where they were able to locate twelve coal barges that had been sunk in the bay off Point Judith, Rhode Island, during last winter's storms.

When the new winter arrived, the vessel was taken out of service and safely moored in a protected harbor in Newport, Rhode Island. A local contractor by the name of John K. Sullivan was Captain Blix's business partner in the coal salvaging enterprise and took charge of the ship throughout the winter. Tied up at a dock since early January, the vessel was laid up and prepared for a period of inactivity during the cold season, when waterways usually freeze.

At this time, the steamboat freighter was twenty-six years old and slowly beginning to show her wear. She was nearing the end of her projected working lifespan, which typically runs from twenty-five to thirty years, for that kind of vessel. Considering all these facts, she had lived a valuable and productive life despite sailing through a few difficult historical events in a time laden with conflicts.

Its final dramatic chapter occurred on Friday, April 6, 1923, which happened to be right after Easter weekend, but the rapid progression into this dark, mysterious end began a bit earlier. At the time, the United States navigated through a tumultuous period in history and was deep in the throes of the prohibition era. A sense of upheaval carried an overall volatile mood, leading to a dramatic increase in organized crime as well as widespread corruption. It had been four years since the 18th Amendment established a national ban on the manufacture, sale, and transportation of alcoholic beverages. And as is usually the case, when something is prohibited, there are always ways to make it available despite the restrictions.

This was especially tempting and feasible, since the neighboring country, Canada, had a different situation: a short prohibition period from 1918 to 1920, after which the law was removed. The circumstance created a perfectly timed years-long profit-making opportunity to satisfy the sudden, highly in-demand United States market, where a country-wide ban reigned from 1920 all the way until 1933. For thirteen long years, Canada experienced a lucrative boom in the liquor industry and was regularly smuggling the prohibited goods into the United States.

This certainly presented a very tempting and highly profitable opportunity for bootleggers that would load the ships in Canada with high-end contraband alcohol, including Scotch whisky, Canadian blended whiskey, French champagne, and Cuban rum. These heavily laden ships would wait across the border just outside the United States territorial waters. Once darkness and fog descended, the ships would proceed, unseen by the authorities, and then quickly find clever ways to unload the cargo on some quiet stretch of United States coastline.

Desperate times and ongoing economic hardships created a very tempting, massive money-making opportunity for smugglers who were of a dangerous or simply reckless character. And it just so happened that in the sunset of her life, the John Dwight vessel became entangled in that risky business as well. A month earlier, in March of 1923, extra efforts were made to control the increasing number of prohibition-era rumrunners with Coast Guard units on high alert. However, this did not deter the most daring and audacious daredevils from pursuing their line of illegitimate business.

It was barely a week before the Easter weekend when two odd men showed up in the Newport harbor in Rhode Island and approached John K. Sullivan, who was caring for the ship. They claimed there had been a change in ownership of the vessel. The first man introduced himself as Captain Malcolm J. Carmichael and appeared to be an old towboat Captain of Jersey City. He presented some credentials, swiftly took over the ship, and became the leading man in charge. The second man, by the name of Captain John King, was the working skipper from Brooklyn, but it turned out later that they both used false names. Captain Carmichael was a somewhat familiar figure in these parts, but no one seemed to know his first name or much about him, since he always kept his distance.

These two men assertively insisted that the vessel John Dwight was now under their ownership, and without much hesitation, John K. Sullivan gave in to their demands. Only a few days later, a work crew of almost a dozen men showed up to supposedly perform an extensive repair and complete a detailed maintenance process in order to restore the vessel to optimal condition. At least that was what they said about the happenings below the deck.

The men on the boat spoke to no one and kept to themselves with a somewhat elusive, reserved attitude. A few days later, in the middle of the night, the boat quietly slipped out of the harbor and departed. The number of men on board was reportedly around 12, and the newly refurbished John Dwight listed its destination as New York. However, the vessel returned to port shortly thereafter, apparently because of dense fog. But a day later, in the early morning, the men in the harbor noticed that the ship was indeed gone and had obviously quietly moved on during the night, this time successfully.

It eventually anchored in Buzzards Bay in perfect sight of the local coastguard that was situated on Cuttyhunk, the smallest of the Elizabeth Islands. The ship remained there for a few days without any visible happenings. It stood perfectly still, and the few small fishing boats that passed by never saw more than a single man on deck. When they hollered a greeting, there was no response, so it all seemed rather odd and not very friendly. The coastguard observed this seeming standstill, but not much happened, and no one inquired about anything.

A few days later, early in the afternoon, a mailboat carrying post from New Bedford to Cuttyhunk passed the steamer. The mailboat's Captain Loveridge quickly made his way towards the ship since he worried that the vessel was in some kind of distress. But just as soon as he approached, the few men on deck scurried under cover and quickly got out of sight. Captain Loveridge thought that was rather odd, but knew some seamen were not very social. He came alongside the boat and called out to offer help, and after a long while, a rather large and grumpy man finally came up on deck. He claimed to be one of John Dwight's captains but didn't give his name and was eager to get the mailboat out of the way. He seemed rather restless and brushed Captain Loveridge off with a quick explanation that they had some engine problems but were resolving them, so they would be on their way in a few minutes.

This was, of course, said only in an effort to diffuse the attention the anchored ship was causing. What the men on board were doing during his time, God only knows, but they were obviously waiting in suspense. The mailboat's Captain Loveridge clearly noticed that the cargo ship was heavily loaded down with freight, which made the ship even slower. But he just nodded his head, realizing nobody needed or wanted his help, and went on his way to keep on time with the mail delivery.

And sure enough, later on, when the pieces of the puzzle were put together, it became clear just what the suspicious and secretive men were waiting for. Money, and lots of it. Local authorities reported that all was quiet up until the first of April, which happened to be Easter Sunday. A man by the name of John Craven of Rutherford arrived by a small transport vessel and boarded the anchored John Dwight. He carried with him a rather expensive Boston bag, lined with chamois made from a mountain antelope skin. In small towns, people see everything, and this man stood out like a sore thumb, especially with such a fancy bag. And of course, in that extravagant handbag was a seriously large sum of money. Around one hundred thousand dollars, to be exact.

Later, stories surfaced that the crew had already received $125,000 in cash while it waited at the dock. However, that was not all. This New Jersey man came out to the anchored vessel with an additional hundred thousand dollars! Obviously, the prohibited goods onboard were actually sold twice over, to two different parties. Some might consider that a pretty audacious move. John Craven was the man carrying the second payment, but the odd thing was, he never reappeared. In fact, he never again left the vessel. He disappeared below the deck with the fancy bag and all that money, and that was pretty much the end of him. He never resurfaced, so I guess one could say that was his last Easter.

One can only imagine what kind of tension developed on board with a ton of cash and a handful of desperate but obviously well-experienced criminals. John Craven walked into a ticking time bomb, and that cost him his life. Of course, he was no angel; he just happened to play a rather dangerous part. In those days, that kind of money was an impressive stash, the entire sum of two payments equivalent to almost four million dollars in today's currency, so this was no small game, but a rather large and very profitable operation. And once the money was on board, all hell broke loose. But it was more of a quietly hidden, clandestine kind of hell, all happening under the deck of the vessel. Except for the characters involved in the actual fight, no one else saw or heard a darn thing.

That same evening, after John Crave's visit and the secretive money stash drop-off, the John Dwight slowly sailed off. But the night was restless and filled with deadly conflict. The full Moon that occurred a few days ago on Easter Sunday still cast enough light to see one's way in the middle of the night. It wasn't pitch black, so the drama on John Dwight occurred in dim moonlight at a dangerous sea.

As expected, money was the culprit, so one can assume the two captains grabbed the big stash in the bag, but that was most likely not enough for them. They probably wanted the entire sum, which means they were after the money from all the others, which was surely not easily done. There were threats, and a deadly fight occurred since this was a desperate, dark, and dangerous situation, and under the circumstances, every man was for himself. In the end, some were killed right on the spot, and a few remained in hiding somewhere under the deck. And then there was a mysterious group of five crew members that stuck together and tried to get away.

Nobody would know a thing about what was going on and the crew's whereabouts, if it wasn't for the steam freighter Dorchester that passed the vessel right before sunrise the very next morning. It was Friday, April 6th, and this would become John Dwight's final daybreak. Much to their surprise, the Dorchester's captain and crew noticed five men in a lifeboat, quietly but eagerly pulling away from the John Dwight.

It was all a rather odd sight, since two men were at oars and the other three were stacked beneath the thwarts - lifeboat seats, which they did in order to maximize the lifeboat's capacity. Or… perhaps they were hiding. All men were silent as a stone, with stern expressions and in a big, desperate kind of hurry. The two men at oars looked straight ahead, their faces in a strained expression, and the other three stashed under lifeboat seats appeared to be completely still, as if wanting to remain out of sight. Despite this curious encounter, the small group of men on the lifeboat did not in any way communicate with the Dorchester, nor did they ask for help. They just passed each other quietly without any communication whatsoever. It was pretty evident that the group in the lifeboat was clearly very eager to leave the John Dwight and get as far away as possible, so the crew on Dorchester did not get involved and continued on their way.

A few minutes later, at around six o'clock, the officer of the Cuttyhunk Coast Guard station who kept an eye on the horizon spotted the John Dwight through a small, unexpected opening in the morning fog. Suddenly, he noticed a distress signal that appeared to be halfway up its mass and looked like a woolen blanket or oilskin. This was clearly a call for help fashioned in haste. The deadly scuffle under the deck had reached its peak. There was clearly an upheaval, and shortly after, a thick cloud of smoke arose from the deck near the pilot house, the enclosed control center of the vessel that housed the steering wheel and navigation control.

This sudden smoke looked quite alarming, but before the Cuttyhunk Coast Guard knew what happened or could do anything about it, the John Dwight's bow dipped, and within minutes the steamer sank like a stone. The locals immediately sent lifeboats to look for survivors, but to their surprise, not a soul was found. All they noticed were a few bottles and small objects floating on the surface, such as an odd suitcase, an ice chest, and a life preserver stenciled with John Dwight, New York. Everything else sank quickly into the ocean's darkness.

After all, the depth of the sea in that location was well over eighty feet.

It all remained somewhat mysterious until the next day, Saturday, when the local fisherman picked up eight bodies that floated in water among bottles of bootleg ale. Seven were wrapped in life preservers with the name John Dwight clearly written out, so there was no doubt about who the casualties were. It appeared four men were dead by drowning, while others carried wounds that indicated some kind of brutal fight. The eighth man was found alone, lying face down in a lifeboat quite a bit of a distance further away. He was mostly uninjured with a smaller wound in the back of his skull, but had been obviously capable enough to get on the lifeboat and make a desperate effort to escape. It was kind of peculiar that his lifeboat had no oars or oarlocks, so he improvised and made sweeps from inside parts of the boards and worked them with a torn belt that acted as an oarlock.

He must have been desperate beyond words, since he wore his improvised oars out and finally succumbed to exhaustion. The wound to his head surely played a role in his demise as well. It appeared that he fell to the bottom of the lifeboat and most likely perished from tiredness in addition to drowning in the water at the bottom of the leaking lifeboat. There was a cheese knife on the crimson-stained deck beside his body, so one can only guess what happened there. It proved to be a sad and tragic end for the young man, later identified as Captain King's son, Henry.

As was the usual procedure, all bodies were taken ashore and properly identified by the papers that they carried in their clothing. One man was older, another was a war veteran with a large tattoo of Harriet on his right forearm. Two men were of unusual height, one smaller and one quite tall, but both were of a younger age. And then there were two bodies that remained unidentified.

Local men who were familiar with the general appearance of both captains could not identify them among the group of drowned bodies, and there was literally no trace of either man, so everything looked increasingly suspect. It certainly appeared that the two captains got away.

Were they the aggressors? It sure seemed that way. But what made it even more dramatic was the terrible shape the dead bodies were in, since they carried fatal injuries. Dukes County Sheriff would later describe their condition as clear evidence of a wicked free-for-all fight. They carried lacerations and bruises about their faces that came from contact with some solid blunt instrument.

Who did this? Were the men fighting back the attacker, were they fighting amongst themselves, or were they caught by complete surprise and remained in shock? After all other victims were identified, there was one last remaining body that was in such a bad shape that it was almost unrecognizable. After much effort, it became clear it belonged to the unfortunate John Craven, the man carrying the Boston bag who brought on board the hefty sum of money. It appeared he met a most brutal end, and one can only imagine the fight he put up and how absolutely volatile his circumstances were. Sad story, about a sad chap with the saddest ending, that's for sure.

All was quiet for a few months until later in June, a group of Navy divers aboard the minesweeper USS Falcon visited the wreck and prepared for exploration as soon as the weather permitted. What they found was crucial and surprising information. The John Dwight was lying on the seafloor and was fully intact, while the deck was loaded with bottles of Frontenac Ale, packed in barrels labeled as flour. The holding area and living quarters were likewise filled with case after case of whiskey.

And then the divers uncovered the most crucial detail. Apparently, the seacock valves that allow seawater in to help cool the engine were open, which was clear evidence of scuttling. It became apparent that the John Dwight was sunk on purpose, by no fault of the ship alone or a wreck of any kind. Nevertheless, it disappeared at the bottom, carrying with it the mystery of its final dramatic hours. Since the vessel carried contraband cargo, the Navy decided to detonate the ship with four depth charges and flatten the site to prevent salvage. Everything seemed a closed matter. One thing was clear: the two captains were never found among the dead, which means they clearly got away. Perhaps they were the ones who scuttled the John Dwight, cold-bloodedly murdered the crew, and swindled them out of the bootlegging profits.

Once again, the small coastline town was eager to put the whole thing behind it, but the shipwreck remained a mystery with much guessing. However, things heated up once again in a little while when the local fisherman eventually found the lifeboat that was met by the passing Dorchester on that fateful morning. It appeared the five men who were departing in such a hurry did in fact manage to get away and landed on a nearby Naushon Island. They successfully escaped and saved their lives, but did they manage to get away with some money? Since the locals also found a new and expensive Boston bag, which was identical to the one used by now perished John Craven, who brought on board all that cash, it certainly appeared as if the group of escapees managed to get away with at least a good portion of the hefty dough.

There was an ongoing search, especially for Captain King, but to no avail. The only report that reached the locals was a fleeting rumor, a few months later, that he was seen in Bermuda. If that was true, he escaped very far, and for that, he most likely also used some of the money gained by this illegal endeavor. He never reappeared and probably hid in Bermuda until his next criminal venture or perhaps simply retired and sat on the sunny beach smoking a pipe till the end of his days. He did have to make peace with the fact that his son lost his life in a criminal episode, and no amount of money was going to bring him back. So, the price for his permanent Bermuda vacation was certainly very high and karmically considerable.

A great deal of speculation continued to swirl about what really happened on John Dwight, and for quite a while the local fisherman insisted there was another story that took place, which is also highly possible since it relies on established and known facts. This version of the story claims that the John Dwight crew hijacked two vessels that were lying low on Rum Row, looted them of money and liquor and left the men to their own devices on a sinking ship. But the saga doesn't end there. Apparently, a larger speedboat that supplied these two smaller vessels with the forbidden cargo, came upon the chaotic event just in time to chase after the John Dwight and eventually catch up with it. The speedboat carried a dangerous and heavily armed crew that attacked the smaller group of men on John Dwight, killed most of them and then deliberately sank the ship.

After the crime, the speedboat hastily left but was badly damaged as well, so it quickly landed not too far away on the East bend of Noman's Land, where it rapidly sank. The crew got off just in time to save their lives and quickly purchased a new, smaller fisherman's boat. The group then turned around, went back to the site of the crime, and a few days later, two rough-looking men appeared and demanded to see the bodies of the sunken John Dwight. When they were granted this request and laid their eyes upon the body of Captain John King's son Harry, they seemed visibly satisfied with the fatal outcome. Harry was the single man in the lifeboat who died from unknown causes, and the men from the speedboat obviously wanted him gone. Perhaps he knew every single one of them and threatened to identify them. It is possible he was even ready to report to the authorities about what had happened. But then again, since he played a part in the original scheme, that wouldn't make much sense.

No matter what the real circumstance was, the two odd men were very content to see Harry dead. They left immediately after viewing his body and never returned. Everything happened so fast and was wrapped in such criminal fog that the authorities simply didn't have the time or the means to detain these two men before they disappeared forever. They were obviously deeply involved and just got incredibly lucky to survive, and then got lucky once again to get away after having the nerve to view Harry's body.

Another rumor came about that a few days after the ship sank, Captain John King suddenly appeared on the island in person and was recognized by a local who had known him for many years. But then the captain just as quickly disappeared and later settled in Bermuda. To add to the puzzling mystery, it was only a short while later that a striking and rather expensively dressed woman suddenly appeared on the island and went about asking the local fishermen all sorts of questions regarding the sinking of John Dwight, which made the men suspiciously silent and uncooperative. The woman did not share a reason for her inquiries and behaved so secretively and yet curiously that the fishermen simply avoided her, and she got very little, if any, information she was searching for. Perhaps she was looking for a man who had disappeared, maybe even John Craven himself, who carried all that cash. Maybe all she wanted was that loaded Boston bag full of dough. And of course, she could have been a fancy bootlegger herself.

Either way, another twelve long years went by before another attempt at searching the shipwreck's remains of John Dwight was made in June of 1935. The Prohibition Era was over, and the locals wanted another crack at solving the John Dwight mystery. A small group of exploratory expedition took another glimpse at the wreckage at the bottom of the sea. They suspected and probably hoped some money was still locked away in a safe compartment that perhaps survived the detonation years ago. But to their surprise, they discovered that the charges had missed their mark, and the old John Dwight was remarkably intact.

After a few dives, the main diver reported that he was able to make a thorough examination of the ship's hull, which was entirely clean and had perfectly intact portions. The detonation years before did, in fact, not damage it at all. The boiler room was damaged with one side forced off, which most likely caused the smoke that the Cuttyhunk Coast Guard saw before the ship sank. There were no traces of any bodies, and everything else seemed relatively unscathed. There was also no sign of any money, and despite the fact that at one time John Dwight undoubtedly carried a large sum of cash on board, there was surely none left of it now.

A month later, the diving exploration team uncovered further elements to help solve the mystery. The main diver reported that, up to his shoulders, the entire cargo space was filled with empty beer bottles and rotted barrel staves. They were in the thousands, and yet not a single bottle of whiskey. The divers were going to keep at it since the whiskey bottles were usually packed in flour barrels, below the beer. The team had to remove all empty beer bottles, which was quite a workload. The sea didn't subsume all of the illicit cargo, so the locals handed the floating barrels stuffed with half-pint bottles of Montreal-brewed Frontenac ale, packed in straw, over to the Coast Guard, which stored it in a warehouse on Martha's Vineyard. It took less than two days before barrels started to go missing, obviously ending up in the local liquor cabinets.

The one interesting final find was the one and only weapon, a two-foot-long knife that was left in the hold, in the deep, below-deck space at the lower part of the hull. Since the ship was resting at about eighty-five feet underwater, the expedition was challenging to say the least. This concluded the first major exploration into John Dwight's final journey. She remained on the seafloor for a few decades, keeping her unfortunate secrets to herself, forever silenced by the mystery of the sea.

*The wheel from John Dwight,
Photo by Arnie Carr*

The wheel from John Dwight lifted to trailer in preparation for transport, Photo by Arnie Carr

By the time I got to view this old, distressed, and mysterious vessel up close, it was half a century later. I must say much remained the same and seemingly untouched. The sea life embraced its new relic and ornamented the vessel with natural decorative elements, so the John Dwight appeared at peace with her dark past. Perhaps because no bodies were ever found on the ship, and it did not really suffer through an aggressive shipwreck hell.

The vessel simply sank and descended as if someone had put her to sleep after years of good and reliable service. At the time of sinking, it was heavily loaded, so it wasn't hard to make it happen. In a way, I could almost feel it let go with a big sigh of relief, as if it was too tired of carrying so much weight and always under strenuous circumstances. John Dwight did not have an easy life, and her ending was not gracious, but at least she got to land on a soft seabed at the bottom of the ocean.

My interaction with this beauty was of a different nature. She lay as if fast asleep, covered with sea life, while providing nice shelter for smaller creatures. I moved around her kindly and attuned myself to the old story that lingered in the hull. The deck was leaning on its side but looked quite well preserved, and I could easily imagine the last human steps that crossed the wooden floor. The timbers and metal framing lay scattered around, and many old rum and brandy bottles were still intact and even had the corks in them. A lot of the cargo was still there, but the big thing that caught my eye and shined like a brand-new penny was the wheel in the shaft. In the 1890s, steamboats had a large, rotating wheel fitted with paddle blades that pushed against the water to propel the vessel.

The other thing I noticed was this big brass propeller with a six-inch brass shaft, and my mind started working, so I mentioned it to Arnie.

"You know we could probably salvage that propeller."

My idea seemed to intrigue him.

"Well, how are we going to get it off? Are we going to cut it off? That'll take forever!" was Arnie's concern.

"No, I got a better idea of how we're going to get that propeller off."

I knew exactly how to get it done. Remember, I had a blaster's license and was licensed to buy and use explosives in Massachusetts, so I actually told Arnie how we could do this. "I learned a trick or two from the North Vietnamese on how to make a satchel charge."

I smiled at Arnie, and he laughed with his hearty laugh.

I said, "No, I'm serious!"

It was not unusual to try and revive a piece of useful material and create something new from a ship's valuable remains. So, Arnie and I decided the wheel might be an ideal piece to revive and repurpose.

I didn't spend a lot of time on the old beauty, but rigging the wheel was the big thing. I just rigged the charge, and that's when Arnie took the photographs. Then I blew that wheel right off the end of the shaft, and we salvaged it and sold it for scrap after I cut the blades off it. But the neat part of that story was that once we got the propeller back to my place in East Venice, I knocked the end of the shaft off, which would have been the locking cap to keep the propeller on the shaft. On the back of it was written USS Pawnee YT-21. So, I felt an interesting unspoken connection with the spirit of the old vessel that worked for the United States Armed Forces, just as I did in my past.

We used Arnie's skiff — a small, shallow, open boat- to do the salvage, and when I set the charge, he was a bit worried that I would blow some of the cotton out of the hull plates, since his vessel had a wooden hull. So, he left me alone, and I quickly blew the wheel off, and all was well, and his vessel thankfully remained intact. He then came back, and we anchored up and discussed how we were going to get the propeller up onto his boat. We ended up using lift bags to hoist it up and latched it right to the back of his boat, which put the stern way down in the water. Then we motored a short distance to East Falmouth, where we got some help with raising the propeller out and then placed it on a trailer that I had borrowed from the marina where I had my shop. Later on, I towed it back to East Dennis and cut the wheels off the blades with a broco rod, a carbon arc gouging rod that can cut, melt, or liquify most materials, and sold it.

The following day, Arnie and I talked about the next exciting project that we were going to pursue. By salvaging John Dwight's old propeller, we preserved the ship's heartbeat so it could go on and exist in another manifestation. It is not lying forgotten at the bottom of the sea, and who knows, perhaps the brass was used for a new ship or even a plane. The rest of John Dwight was left in peace to rest amongst the wondrous sea life for eternity, as a reminder of a time in history when life was very different than today.

Captain Joseph Amaral Jr. repairing the rigging to lift sheep's wheel from John Dwight, Photo by Arnie Carr

*Mrs. William K. Vanderbilt in her costume
of a "Venetian Renaissance Lady" at the Vanderbilt Ball
held at 660 Fifth Avenue, on March 26, 1883
Photo by José Maria Mora (1847-1926)
Library of Congress*

Chapter Three

THE GILDED AGE BEAUTY

The Luxurious Alva

LOCATION: *Cape Cod, Massachusetts*
WATER DEPTH: *approximately 50 feet*
DATE OF SHIPWRECK: *July 24, 1892*
CAUSE: *Collision with the steamer H.F. Dimock in dense fog*
PASSENGERS: *Five passengers and 52 crew members*
SURVIVORS: *Everyone survived*

Let's begin this interesting story where it's proper, with its name. This stunning luxury yacht was named after Alva, one of the Gilded Age's most calculating and remarkable women. She was the first wife of the mighty William K. Vanderbilt, who was born into incredible wealth as the grandson of the legendary railroad tycoon Cornelius Vanderbilt.

Alva came into this world on January 17, 1853, in Mobile, Alabama. Her father, Murray Smith, stemmed from a prominent family of Scottish origin and was a lawyer who eventually became a wealthy American commission merchant, planter, and landowner. Her mother, Phoebe, likewise came from a powerful, politically well-connected family and was famous for hosting costly but rather unpopular parties. Alva grew up with a few siblings but lost two very early on, so altogether only three sisters remained, with Alva being the youngest. The family led a very comfortable, privileged life and owned a number of slaves. Their advantageous position allowed them to move between Newport, Rhode Island, and luxurious summer trips to Europe, where they indulged in entertaining and socializing.

Their lives were seemingly carefree until the threat of Civil war, which clearly indicated that times were about to change rather drastically. Alva's father, Murray, quickly decided to move the family to New York City, and when the Civil War fully broke out in 1861, the family relocated to Europe in order to gain distance from the upheaval and avoid the conflict at home. The next setback was obvious when the lucrative cotton trade was suddenly cut, and the family's great fortune slowly but steadily began to evaporate. The family lived in Paris for a few years, where Alva attended private schools, and after the war ended in 1865, they had no choice but to return to New York, where they quickly faced total financial ruin. Their social standing was all they had left, but the family fortune was tragically lost, and the stressful situation heavily affected the entire household. They were thrown into a difficult circumstance with no actual abilities to manage and thrive.

In order to make ends meet, Alva's mother, Phoebe, was forced to run a boarding house, while her father, Murray, worked as a cotton broker. The struggle was gut-wrenching and lasted six long and turbulent years, when in 1871, Alva's mother suddenly died at barely forty-nine years of age. The loss of her mother was an existential shock, and Alva, who just turned eighteen, had to rely on her inventiveness to help keep the family together. She was a strong and willful young woman who was perfectly aware that the only way to rescue herself and her family was to swiftly marry a wealthy husband. She was naturally very social and used her good education as her one and only advantage. For four years, she struggled and tried to keep her family's social connections alive and as advantageous as possible.

And finally, her luck arrived. As fate would have it, her best girlfriend by the name of Consuelo Montagu, also known as the Duchess of Manchester, invited Alva to a glamorous private party for one of Henry Vanderbilt's daughters. It was at that event that the young twenty-two-year-old Alva was introduced to William Kissam Vanderbilt, a well-groomed and savvy son of Henry Vanderbilt. Alva's sparkling personality, international flair, and obvious intellect quickly won him over, while his elevated demeanor and tremendous fortune were a most attractive prospect for desperate Alva. The young bachelor was only four years older, and they seemed a perfect match.

Alva felt she hit the absolute jackpot, and the lovebirds did not waste much time. They married less than a year later, on April 20, 1875, in New York City. Naturally, the wedding was a major social event and was considered a huge affair in New York society. Barely two weeks after the wedding, Alva's very ill father passed away, so she was suddenly left without parents and never forgot how they suffered in harsh poverty at their very end. This made her even more acutely aware of her own great fortune to have married so exceptionally well, just in the nick of time to avoid a sure financial catastrophe and total ruin.

With her new husband, her own family's name was swiftly recovered, social standing repaired, and bankruptcies avoided. Alva and William embarked on a socially active marriage and had three children: a first-born daughter and two boys. Once the family unit was well established, Alva felt absolutely secure in her powerful social standing. Naturally, incredibly confident and well-equipped to assert her position in New York City's upper class, she reveled in throwing grand balls and paving the way with her clear ambition to build an influential position at the top of the high society. She usually thought well ahead and began focusing on securing the future prominent marriages of her three children. She cultivated a razor-sharp eye for the assets and position of all prospective partners.

Perhaps old memories of her family's traumatic past experience with shaky finances left her traumatized, and she carried a deep anxiety and urge to ensure she would never suffer like that again. It truly seemed that insurmountable wealth and high social standing were a great and possibly only comfort to her. In 1886, when her husband inherited sixty-five million from his father's estate, Alva quickly set her sights on a new luxury project. She announced that she wanted to own a yacht. This was not her husband's idea, but very clearly her ambition and obsession to simply outdo everyone else.

In order to satisfy Alva's newest whim, her husband William K. Vanderbilt commissioned the steel luxury ship in 1886 and had it built in Wilmington, Delaware, by the Harlan & Hollingsworth Company. This extravagant steamship, which cost $500,000 to construct, was specially designed by a British designer from Liverpool by the name of St. Caere Bayre, who sent two of his best assistants to help with the construction. The ship was a floating palace, and the grandiose extravagance was a mighty display of Vanderbilt's endless wealth.

Very appropriately and to his wife's great joy, the fancy yacht was named after Alva herself and was considered the most luxurious yacht of its time. At 285 feet in length, it was the largest private vessel in the world at the time of its completion.

*William K. Vanderbilt,
Bain News Service publisher
Library of Congress*

It was a three-masted schooner, and the hull was of finest quality mild steel. The tonnage was 1,151.27 or 600.55 net, and the entire ship was lit throughout with electricity.

Massive frames that thickly ribbed the vessel were of plate steel, as was the floor and deck. Three powerful and mighty engines furnished the propelling power that operated through a propeller wheel, which was a splendid, solid cast, manganese bronze four-bladed screw that weighed ten thousand pounds. Like most of the things on board, this too was made abroad. The yacht deck was fitted with three steel-plated cabins, the first one able to communicate with the main saloon and Mr. Vanderbilt's own apartments that included eight separate rooms altogether. Furthermore, the ship boasted elaborately exquisite cabins, a richly decorated parlor that included a fancy card room. In addition, the ship had a library, smoking room, and seven spacious guest chambers, all adorned in white enamel and gold. The extraordinarily fancy equipment onboard included a self-leveling dining table that assured an uninterrupted dinner for the guests, regardless of how rough the seas might get that the ship might possibly encounter.

Once the ship's construction was completed, it was ready to sail in October of 1886 and quickly became the Queen of the New York Yacht Club's Fleet. The family invited a few selected friends and embarked on extensive travels, including long voyages to the Caribbean and Europe. This glorious specimen of a ship required fifty-five crew members just to man the complex and mighty craft.

The first extended cruise was made in July of 1887, when the Vanderbilt family traveled across the Atlantic, all the way to the Mediterranean and then further on to the Nile and then returned back home by way of the Canary Islands and Nassau. The family and friends entertained themselves with various endeavors, including collecting unusual marine specimens intended for growing a natural history museum.

The following big trip occurred two years later in the fall of 1889, when Alva returned to Europe and visited several ports, then spent winter in Nice, in the South of France, and cruised among the West Indian Islands on the way back home. On this particular journey, Vanderbilt had the intention to sail around the world, but then abruptly changed his mind. Perhaps something bothered him? Maybe the close friendship his wife was displaying with one of his close friends?

There were many personal friends who accompanied the Vanderbilts on these extravagant and long journeys, and through these numerous entertaining travels, Alma met her husband's friends, including his good friend Oliver Hazard Belmont. It was a friendship that quickly grew unusually close since Alva was not happy in her marriage. Belmont accompanied the Vanderbilts on at least two of these long voyages aboard their yacht. It was rather evident that he and Alva were attracted to one another upon their return from one such voyage in 1889. Clearly, William K. Vanderbilt could not watch this obvious fond interaction between his wife and his best friend happening right in front of his eyes, while enduring the awkward situation all the way around the world. So he cut the trip short, just like that.

As always, it was not just Alva who was looking for comfort elsewhere; in fact, before this happened, it became well known that William K. Vanderbilt was finding entertainment elsewhere and was cheating on his wife with none other than Alva's best friend, who originally introduced the Vanderbilts to each other years ago. Yes indeed, it was the Duchess of Manchester, Consuelo Yznaga, who became William's intimate new friend, and it became quite apparent that the Vanderbilt marriage seemed to be hitting a rough patch or perhaps a fatal wreck! Perhaps these uncomfortably awkward escapades of betrayal somehow influenced the yacht's sudden spell of bad fortune.

On a return from a long cruise in 1891, the ship steamed into New York harbor with the Vanderbilts and their entire entourage crowded as far forward as possible, while a yellow flag flew at the main mast. The Yellow Jack flag indicated the presence of disease and was most unbecoming for Alma's passengers and their stature. But they were people like everyone else, mere mortals vulnerable to disease. It seemed that misfortune met one of the crew members, a sailor, who caught smallpox while on the cruise, and the entire Vanderbilt party was beside themselves. One can only imagine their fright while being stuck on a ship with a highly contagious person! No fancy jewelry could be helpful there! It goes without saying that the vessel went into quarantine and had to remain offshore, while no one was allowed to board or leave the vessel until health officials granted a clean bill of health. Surely not very comfortable for people who usually did anything they wished or desired.

Another unfortunate incident occurred a year later, on the afternoon of June 11, 1892, when the yacht ran into a rowboat in North River. A romantic couple was enjoying a summer outing when they got struck by Alva and both instantly perished. Aboard the yacht was only Mr. Vanderbilt and his usual party of gentlemen. Apparently, the lines on the yacht made it very difficult to do a sudden turn, and the two people in the rowboat got rather panicked before the unfortunate accident occurred. It was a tragic event, and one wonders how it affected the small group on board. Did they just continue with the card games? Perhaps drank a bit more to soothe the drama?

And finally, the spell of misfortune came to a head when Alva was on her final voyage and endured a fatal crash. It just shows to prove that despite her massive beauty and opulent design, Alva was just like any other vessel, vulnerable to accidents and easily destroyed.

It all happened on a seemingly carefree Sunday, on July 24, 1892, to be precise. The yacht was anchored in Cape Cod when it unexpectedly collided with the freight steamer H.F Dimock and then tragically sank. Dimock, that originally left the company's dock at Pier 11 in North River at six o'clock on Saturday night was lightly loaded with freight and bound for Boston on what expected to be a twenty-hour trip. The captain and twenty-seven officers in the crew made their way to Boston, where they were expected at one in the afternoon on Sunday.

Meanwhile, William K.Vanderbilt was onboard his yacht Alva with his brother, Frederick, and five male guests for a stag party. Due to the bad weather that completely cut off all observation, the Alva crew decided to anchor down and wait it out. Everything was enveloped in dense fog when they were suddenly awakened by a tremendous crash of the collision at 3:20 in the morning. Alma's captain was horrified at the sight of a massive American-built 300-foot steamer of 2,625 gross tons that struck the yacht broadside, eight feet from the stern, plowing its way several feet across the deck and crushing in the bow plates well below the water line.

The water poured through the aperture in torrents, and merely a few minutes after the collision, the bow began to settle. It became quickly and undoubtedly clear that the marvelous yacht was fatally wounded. The fifty-two Alva's crew members worked in perfect unison and quickly prepared the five lifeboats for the passengers and crew. William K.Vanderbilt and his friends were swiftly brought on deck and assisted to safely leave the wreck. There was not a minute to lose, and no one had any time to pack a thing. They left with what they wore on their backs and were lucky to get out unhurt. In a few minutes, they found themselves on H.F Dimock, safely rescued and well taken care of.

One of the firemen was ordered into Alva's boiler room to tend to the fires, which he promptly did; however, upon his return on deck, he noticed he was the very last person remaining on board, while everyone else had departed onto the freight ship. Beautiful Alva was plunging with rapid speed, her nose already underwater, and stern going upwards since the bow was carried down by the weight of the water, which rapidly filled the forward compartment. The decks were awash, and since the fireman was left behind, he had no other option but to jump ship. He bravely plunged into the sea and was thankfully quickly pulled aboard the steamer's deck. All were rescued safely and cheered in gratitude. Then everyone grew eerily quiet, as they observed in horror and fear how the last of the luxurious beauty sank below the surface in mere fifteen minutes. The drama was intense, and William K.Vanderbilt and his few friends had a moment of deep reflection. All their wealth did not matter one bit when death brushed so near; they could feel its cold breath.

William K. Vanderbilt thought of his wife and was grateful she was spared this frightful episode, but on the other hand, he suddenly regretted that they led such separate lives. Their marriage was in trouble for some time, and they barely saw each other. At the time of the shipwreck, Alva was at their newly built summer home, Marble House, in Newport, Rhode Island. It seemed they both entertained other people and ceased to entertain each other.

When Alva received the news about the shipwreck and the yacht's demise, she went into her room, closed the door behind her, and sat down in front of her dressing table. Then she took a long, hard look at herself in the mirror. A serious, cold face was looking back at her. She was this close to losing her William, and yet, she could not shed a tear. The betrayals, adultery, coldness, and embarrassment in society for his ignorant behavior towards her had done their work. She felt no love, not a thing. Nevertheless, she was relieved to hear everyone was saved, despite the fact that the marriage was coming to an end. William and Alva were clearly growing apart, and with the sunken yacht that carried her name, it felt almost like a symbolic connection to their sunken, irreparable marriage.

There was much debate in the papers about what had happened, and an admiralty court later found that Alva was at fault for the collision, as it had anchored improperly in the fog-filled Pollock Rip Channel. The shipwreck site was pretty much left alone except for the usual procedure of using dynamite, blowing it to bits, and sending it to the bottom of the sea. If left untouched, it would present a great hazard to navigation in the busy shipping lanes.

As usual, when facing any material loss, William K. Vanderbilt did not fret much or for long. To him, everything and just about everyone was replaceable, so barely a few hours later, as soon as he reached the shore, he immediately ordered the construction of a new yacht. This new steam yacht was going to be named the Valiant, and it belonged to him and later to his brother Frederic.

As usual, Vanderbilt simply rapidly moved on, erasing the accident and plowing forward with his luxurious and busy lifestyle.

Three years after the shipwreck in March of 1895, Alva shocked society when she decided to finally divorce William K. Vanderbilt. It was an unusual and daring decision for those times, but she was confident and strong and eventually walked away with a more than ten-million-dollar settlement, which would be about 380 million in today's currency. She also received a few estates and was well set up for the rest of her life. Her reasoning for divorce was Vanderbilt's relentless adultery and open relationship with her best friend, Consuelos.

Only a few months later, on January 11, 1896, Alva remarried Vanderbilt's old friend Oliver Belmont in a very small, quiet ceremony held at her home. Only a few friends were present, with the mayor officiating the ceremony. Oliver Belmont was six years her junior and had a rather difficult past experience in his previous marital life a decade earlier. He went through a very public and bitter divorce, followed by a custody battle and eventual disownment of his child, all prompted by his gambling, drinking, addiction, and consequential adultery. Nevertheless, Alva and Oliver became close confidants through the years when they met at social gatherings as well as on Alva's extraordinary world journeys, and seemed quite compatible together.

She gave the relationship a chance, and they remained married over ten years, until his sudden death in 1908, caused by appendicitis. He was barely forty-nine years old, and the grief-stricken Alva Vanderbilt Belmont immediately left for Europe. She returned to the States a year later in 1909, when she took on the new cause and generously dedicated her fortune to the women's suffrage movement while establishing eleven suffrage settlements across the New York City area. In 1913, Alva urged that women be given voting rights within the Episcopal Church and eventually became the president of the National Woman's Party. Her ex-husband, William K. Vanderbilt, passed on in 1920, and from then on, Alva lived in Paris until her death in 1933 at the age of eighty.

Two years before she died in 1931, Alva's beloved son, William K. Vanderbilt II. commissioned a new, even larger state-of-the-art motor yacht. It was designed for extensive global expeditions and was named Alva in honor of his dear mother.

And now, we've arrived at the point, my dear reader, where the past meets the present. My meeting with the glamorous Alva occurred precisely ninety-nine years after she sank. As you can imagine, the location of the shipwreck remained an utter mystery. That is, until, and yes, you guessed it, a team of my great friends and master explorers found it. As you might expect, it was more than tempting to embark on this search. My besties, Arnie Carr and John Fish, were notoriously famous on the Cape for locating shipwrecks. They were tremendous experts and used much research as well as top sonar equipment to uncover the secret location of this precious and luxurious vessel. As we went through this adventure, I truly loved every minute of it.

It was in the early summer of 1981 when John and Arnie "uncovered the queen," as Alva herself would probably say. Let me be clear, this was not a treasure hunt for the Vanderbilt fortune, because there was most likely none on board. It was more or less a historical research journey to see what remained to be recovered of the once-famed beauty. John wanted to discourage scrap salvagers who have no regard for history, and for that reason, even after their find appeared in the newspapers, Arnie and John decided not to disclose the vessel's location. Ever. All that was revealed was that Alva's wreckage rested about sixty miles south of the Cape, since it wrecked on a shoal off Cape Cod.

Once my friends and I arrived at the secret location, I submerged and quickly reached Alva's hiding place. It was pretty clear that a century ago, they successfully blew the yacht to shreds, for reasons well known. It would have presented a serious hazard had they left it as it was. This was an enormous ship, and they used a whole lot of dynamite to blow it up. Some remains still showed their well-polished design and appearance. I saw a lot of wreckage that was heavily blasted, probably more than once, because there were so many short bits spread all about the wreckage location. But she was still massive, so large in fact, that one could not see the end of it. She was lying on the sea bottom, and a lot of it was actually in the sand.

The first thing I noticed was an enormous number of relatively large lobsters everywhere, which was kind of amusing. It almost seemed as if they were protecting their beloved domain that was there for their exclusive enjoyment. Now, a disturbance was occurring with our uninvited presence, so they quickly moved away into hiding, still carefully keeping an eye on the unwelcome intruders.

The first time I dove underwater, I didn't really get a lot of time to actually look at the wreck in greater detail and explore what was there, because I had a very specific mission. John had already examined the wreckage previously and wanted to recover the capstan, which is a heavy rotating machine, often with a vertical drum, used for hauling heavy ropes, cables, or chains by winding them around a central cylinder. This particular capstan was on the bow, so it was primarily used to bring up the anchor. In those days, the capstans were usually made of wood or iron, and even a combination of both. Well, not this one. It was made of solid brass. Who does that with a capstan? Obviously, Vanderbilt, because he could. But I must say, it was beautiful.

I had to blow the capstan off, which I did with a detonating cord, and thankfully it didn't break. The other interesting item was the engraved builder's plaque, also called a maker's plate, which is a durable, unique identification plate, and at that historical time period, it was usually made of cast brass or bronze. The plaque serves as the shipbuilder's permanent signature and the vessel's birth certificate, so it is a vital recovery item. The builder's plate on Alva was made of solid brass and truly looked quite impressive. We also recovered a stateroom window, but one final item was particularly interesting to us, and that was the porthole.

A porthole on an old ship is an unusual, round or oval window set in the hull of the ship. It is, of course, used for getting some light into the cabin, and if the weather at sea is good, a porthole is excellent for enjoying the sea view as well as ventilating the cabin with some fresh air. This unique window has a strong design that holds very thick glass, which can withstand the sea pressure while staying tight with no leaks or stress points. When a porthole is closed shut, it remains very tight, and during a storm, it is covered with a heavy cover and locked with massive bolts.

So the three of us embarked on the search for portholes. We anchored up, and because the tide runs so hard in that specific location, we had to wait for a low tide before diving in. I jumped in on an early tide and used a grappling hook, which is a multi-pronged hook attached to a rope, designed to catch and grip surfaces. And right next to where the grappling hook held its grip, there was a whole row of portholes with blackout covers. It was on the right, the starboard side of the ship, where the cabins used to be.

They were the finest portholes that the Vanderbilt family could have purchased. Looking gorgeous and made of solid brass, they still held onto the iron hull. Since they were so close to the anchor, I assumed I could take the porthole off very easily and would just tie it onto the anchor. Then we would pull on the hook, and easily also remove the porthole.

Well, my friend John came down behind me and said he'd prefer to work on that specific porthole himself. And he began diligently and carefully working on that one porthole. Instead of waiting around, I swam all the way to the other

side of the line with all the portholes and easily knocked off a porthole on the very end. It was rather effortless, and very quick since I just used a pry bar and placed it into the spot where the porthole was held onto the side of the ship. The massive steel bolts that held it in place had deteriorated enough, so all it took was two easy hits with a sledgehammer into my pry bar. By just placing a bit of weight on it, all the bolts immediately snapped out, and the porthole got loose.
I brought it back to where John was still working on his one porthole. I threw it down on the seafloor, while he looked up and said:

"Huh, okay."

It was all quite funny. Then I went down to the end of the line again, and I did the same thing, and brought him another porthole in a matter of minutes. And he was still working on that first porthole, slowly and carefully, with very little progress. Moments later, I brought him the third one and placed it down next to the anchor, and now he was really paying attention.

I went back again to the end of the line, snapped off the fourth one, and brought it back to the anchor. By that time, he almost had his one porthole off.

I was kneeling at the bottom of the sea, watching John work, and trying to figure out how I'm going to hook up these portholes that I got free, so we could lift them up with the anchor, because now it was obviously going to be quite a heavy load.

In the meantime, John finally got his one and only porthole off, and we rigged all of them to the line and pulled them all up. It took the strength of three strong men to lift them up since we didn't have a captain on board and had to do it by hand. We gathered our forces and pulled them all up, and once we finally got them onboard, we just sat there, wiped out, looking at these massive brass portholes. I still have the one I first found, with the blackout cover pulled down. It must weigh at least forty pounds, the glass is extraordinarily thick, but what makes it so heavy is the blackout cover. It is a treasure, that is for sure.

What fascinates me to this day are the endless possibilities of different, unusual people that peeked through that porthole when the beautiful Alva was still intact and sailing away through the world's most beautiful seas and various ports.

Who was looking through this porthole? Was it Alva herself? Was she with her husband, William Vanderbilt, sharing her joy when first boarding the luxurious vessel? How long did that thrill last, perhaps a few days or months?

Obviously, later on, while traveling on the long journeys with selected friends, Alva first got close to her future second husband, Oliver Belmont, precisely on this ship. Did she look out at sea through this porthole while seeking comfort in Oliver and confided to him her marital misery?

And then there's also the interesting fact that William Vanderbilt himself took numerous short journeys on this yacht, not with his wife but with his gentleman friends when he entertained them with various stag parties and such. I imagine they probably smoked fancy cigars late into the night, played cards, and had a bit too much to drink.

Were they truly alone? Was his wife's best girlfriend and his new romantic interest, Consuelos, with him? Did this porthole see William captivating and charming her into his seductive and irresistibly powerful web of insurmountable wealth? We shall never know.

The porthole is almost like an old mirror that saw and reflected the images of fascinating people in the faraway past. But everything the window saw is forever kept a secret. The window between the mysterious dimensions of time is like the very eye of the ship. Everything it observed in a time long ago and far away remains a sea-flavored mystery, forever locked away in history.

The porthole from the Alva.
Photo by Captain Joseph Amaral Jr.

*The salvage vessel for recovery of Brother Jonathan
Photo by Captain Joseph Amaral Jr.*

Chapter Four

THE FORTUNE HUNTERS

The Golden Treasure on Brother Jonathan

LOCATION: *A few miles Southwest of Point St. George, off the coast of Crescent City, California*
WATER DEPTH: *275 Feet*
DATE OF SHIPWRECK: *July 30, 1865*
CAUSE: *hitting an uncharted rock during a severe storm*
PASSENGERS: *244 souls on board, passengers and crew*
SURVIVORS: *19 survivors, 225 perished*

In the mid-nineties, I was approached to work on a recovery mission involving the legendary shipwreck of a paddle steamer named the S.S. Brother Jonathan. This vessel sank off the coast of California and went down as the deadliest wreck on the Pacific Coast up to that time. It claimed over two hundred lives, and only a small group of nineteen people survived. It was a tragedy of the ages, and what made matters worse was the fact that there was no proper recovery of the mighty ship. It simply disappeared into the depths of the Pacific Ocean. Before I share with you my fascinating experience with this dramatic shipwreck, here is the story of the historic vessel and her journey.

The steamer was made on the East Coast in Williamsburg, Brooklyn, by Perrine, Patterson, and Stack, and first launched in November 1850. At 220 feet in length and 36 feet in width, it was a rather imposing ship commissioned by Edward Mills from New York. The name Brother Jonathan stemmed from a fictional character, developed as a good-natured parody of New England during the early American Republic.

The historical period from 1848 until 1855 was the time of the great California Gold Rush, and the massive migration westward created a major boom in the shipping business. The unprecedented demand for sea transport inspired new routes and created a thriving enterprise for many. There were three primary paths to get to California, of course, by land; second, by ship in a long journey around Cape Horn; and then there was the third option via the Panama Route. This was the journey Brother Jonatan undertook and initially set a record for the fastest round-trip in thirty-one days. The ship would sail from New York through the Atlantic Ocean's side to the long isthmus in Panama, which was one of the most significant headlands in the world and presented a risky option. The passengers with their cargo would then journey across the land and finally board another vessel to continue traveling north towards California on the Pacific Ocean's side.

In 1852, a mere two years after the steamer was built, the new owner became no other than Cornelius Vanderbilt, an American industrialist and shipping magnate who was one of the wealthiest men in America. He purchased the steamer to replace one of his wrecked ships and selected the primary and safer route for the journeys to California via Cape Horn. He also used it on the West Coast side of the Pacific Ocean for the remainder of the route. In order to make more room for passengers and increase the profits, he greatly expanded the steamer and created a relatively comfortable upscale vessel.

Next, he explored an additional route for a shorter travel time and ferried passengers across the isthmus through Nicaragua, which was a more than six hundred miles or approximately two days shorter way to California. But in 1856, the Nicaraguan government cancelled the agreement, and Vanderbilt quickly turned his interests towards the railway on the East Coast.

Later on, the ship was sold and renamed Commodore, the new owner, Captain John T. Wright, who moved it to his home port of San Francisco, from where it sailed to British Columbia. There was a great demand for travel by many new prospectors who wanted to reach Fraser Canyon, a very promising new location for gold mining. In a few years, the vessel began showing its age, and in 1861, it was sold yet again to new owners, the California Steam Navigation Company. They spared no expense for significant upgrades and restored it to the original name of Brother Jonathan.

The refurbished vessel was truly luxurious in appearance with ornamented paneling and gold leaf decorative embellishments, spacious first-class cabins, and plenty of space for large numbers of passengers, in addition to an enormous room for cargo. It became known as the fastest ship to travel the regular route from San Francisco, through Portland, all the way up to Vancouver in a record sixty-nine hours in one direction.

In early spring of 1862, a widespread tragedy occurred when a passenger infected with smallpox boarded the ship. He was a gold miner traveling up north, but unfortunately, his presence caused a rapid spread of the disease amongst other passengers and eventually indigenous people. The mass migration at that time brought along the foreseeable challenges and dangers to the indigenous people. The colonials forced the untreated indigenous people to leave Victoria, but this only accelerated the massive spread of illness, which wiped out around thirty thousand people and left behind utter devastation, deserted villages, and traumatized a small remnant of the indigenous population, while the colonization of the area dramatically escalated.

A few years later, in early June 1865, the vessel suffered a collision with a schooner bark on the Columbia River. The impact was serious enough that it considerably damaged the hull, which was suddenly in dire need of repair. The steamer's Captain Samuel DeWolf was a Nova Scotia native with vast experience at sea, as well as one of the few survivors of a serious shipwreck only a few years back. Now he was in command of Brother Jonathan and made a strong point to prevent further damage and properly complete the repairs in dry dock, but the owners ignored his suggestion and insisted on quick repairs while the vessel remained in water, which was far from ideal. The captain was not happy about it, but there was not much he could do.

This one unfortunate, smaller accident that caused damage to the hull was perhaps only a prelude and a sign of the things to come. Along with Captain DeWolf were his First Officer Allen, Second Officer Campbell, and a tall Black quartermaster, Yates. Before the departure of the ill-fated journey, Captain DeWolf voiced his concern about the overloading of the vessel, which took over twelve hours, resulting in the steamer being literally packed to the hilt.

On board was a great fortune, crates of gold bars and coins, massive jewels, barrels of whiskey, and an immensely heavy quartz-gold ore crusher that weighed a few tons. The heavy machinery was an essential piece of equipment and was used to break down crystal and recover gold. Some of the gold onboard was a Wells Fargo shipment consigned for Portland and Vancouver. There was also a large sum in gold specifically intended to pay the troops and cover the annual treaty payments for the Indian tribes. This was obviously very important cargo in addition to the ship's safe and carefully kept Purser's inventory of all the goods. The gold alone was valued at $50 million in today's dollars.

But what mattered more than anything were the hopeful souls on board, counting around 244 passengers altogether, looking forward to creating a new life for themselves or joining their family, relatives, and loved ones up the coast. The travelers were a very colorful group, including hopeful settlers, enthusiastic prospectors, freed slaves, and an impressive company of dignitaries. Brigadier General George Wright, who was the past commander of the Pacific for the Union Forces, was traveling to Fort Vancouver to take on a new post. With his wife Margaret at his side, they both looked forward to the new chapter of their lives. On the journey was also William Logan, newly appointed superintendent of the Dallas Mint in Oregon.

And then there was Governor Anson G. Henry of the Washington territory, who had an especially challenging time as he just lost his good friend, President Abraham Lincoln, only a few months ago. He was the president's personal physician and was just returning from offering support to Lincoln's widow after the dramatic loss of her beloved husband. There were a few more military personnel travelers, as well as James Nibet, a well-known author and part-owner of the San Francisco Bulletin. Another interesting and unusual passenger was Mrs. Jeannete Lee, a young wife of a prominent Circus owner in Portland. She was a horse rider in her husband's show extravaganza that had moved to Vancouver and carried the payroll for the entire circus cast and crew. A brand-new mother, she traveled with her three-week-old baby, two camels, and her favorite show horse. In addition, there were other precious animals that traveled as well, a few horses and a Newfoundland dog.

And then there was another unusual traveler, namely Mrs. Roseanna Hughes Keenan, a famed San Francisco madam. Dressed in a luxurious coat and dripping with jewels, she was surrounded by her seven most valuable ladies of the evening, adorned in colorful attire and always catching plenty of attention. Madame and her establishment were asked to leave San Francisco, and it was for that reason that her husband, John C. Keenan, traveled ahead some time ago and successfully established a new saloon in Vancouver. The couple was quite wealthy and had owned various hotels and saloons in California, but was recently pushed to sell everything and leave town. So, they set their eyes on Vancouver, which had more relaxed laws and plenty of promising customers in the gold rush industry. The husband was eagerly awaiting his wife and the ladies in Vancouver, and it was for that reason that Mrs. Keenan carried quite a fortune. This was their farewell journey, and she carried their every last cent with her. All the ladies who traveled with her stayed in her private cabin under anonymous names.

On that fated day of Friday, July 28, 1865, Brother Jonathan left the San Francisco Bay and took off on her last journey to Vancouver with a few stopovers, including Portland. The steamer was packed to the hilt, and Captain DeWolf's concerns about an overloaded vessel were quickly proven right when the vessel got stuck in the mud right from the get-go. They were simply forced to wait for the high tide before a tugboat pulled them out so they could sail off with a four-hour delay. The journey proved quite challenging as the steamer ran into enormous winds and monstrous waves that quickly overwhelmed everyone on board. Passengers mostly remained in their cabins, enduring seasickness and chilling fright caused by the dangerously volatile weather.

Captain DeWolf remained calm while navigating the treacherous waters, and to everyone's relief, on Sunday morning, July 30, they finally anchored in the small coastal harbor of Crescent City. They offloaded some of the passengers but were still heavily loaded, and the calm weather only lasted a few hours. They were set to depart that same afternoon to expeditiously move on their journey. Despite seemingly calm weather conditions in the harbor, the captain's decision to leave Crescent City in the middle of a gale of wind was an obvious mistake. The seeming relief in harbor was short-lived since once they returned to the open sea, the stormy conditions suddenly became increasingly volatile, and the steamer endured unmanageably dangerous conditions. By the time they arrived near the Oregon border, Captain DeWolf's intuition was to turn around as soon as possible and return to Crescent City. Everyone onboard was fraught with fear beyond description while the large luxury steamer endured heavy winds and impossible traveling conditions.

The extraordinarily high waves tossed the vessel like a toy, and all passengers were traumatized, seasick, and scared to death. After less than an hour of this uncontrollable torment, the ship neared a dangerous, uncharted reef near Point St. George, and within minutes, the inevitable happened. The steamer struck a rock that caused massive damage to the hull precisely in the area where it had been damaged a few weeks earlier. It did not take long for everyone on board to realize their minutes were numbered and the grave danger was ascending beyond control or hope of salvation. Captain DeWolf quickly ordered that they all immediately abandon the ship. The final ordeal lasted less than an hour and then… the ship was simply gone.

There were plenty of lifeboats, but due to the volatile storm, once they were lowered and filled with passengers, they smashed against the large vessel, sending everyone falling overboard and into the cold water. The first large lifeboat dramatically capsized, and after the second lifeboat smashed into a thousand pieces, no one wanted to board them, and the remaining passengers watched the ordeal and hesitated to descend into the lifeboats themselves. There was only one small surfboat that managed to stay afloat. The strong Quarterman Yates was amongst the crew members in the surfboat pulling at the oars, as well as three Portuguese sailors. This tiny boat carried eleven crew members, five women, and three children. Those were the only remaining survivors out of 244 passengers on board.

Brother Jonathan sank quickly, and within minutes, the large vessel began disappearing into the dark depths of the merciless ocean. Not more than twenty minutes after the small lifeboat managed to gain some distance from the majestic steamer, the sinking vessel completely disappeared. It took the small group of survivors about four hours to return to Crescent City harbor. Once news of the disaster got out, four rescue boats immediately set out to search for survivors. They tried in vain to reach the sinking ship and had to turn around and return home without even a glimpse of the great vessel or any possible survivors. The blasting waves engulfed everything, and Brother Jonathan was simply gone, along with all the passengers. The bodies and various pieces of the broken vessel appeared along the coast for weeks and months after the sinking. It was a most tragic event that shattered the community and the land. Everyone heard of this shipwreck as it marked a very sad and unfortunate chapter in sailing history.

It goes without saying that major efforts were made to recover the wreck, but to no avail. It took over 125 years for that to occur, and this is when I was called to help find and recover the long-sought-after remains of this legendary steamer.

The mighty ship sank a short distance from the coast, about eight miles from Crescent City, but the extremely hazardous coastal environment, filled with dangerous underwater currents and dangerous sharp rocks, as well as a great depth of at least 275 feet, made the recovery just about impossible.

Open diving bell, Photo by Richard Savoy

My meeting with the remains of Brother Jonathan was a powerful experience. It was 1996, more than a century after the tragedy and numerous failed attempts at any kind of recovery. A large team of competent professionals was gathered by my great friend and hero, Harvey Harrington, who was the Deep Sea Research vice president and director of offshore operations. He organized the project's financing and directed the entire complex operation. Every intricate detail of the challenging recovery project was carefully planned and included massive state-of-the-art equipment, as well as Snooper, a two-man small submarine, and an ROV, a deep diving Remote Operated Vehicle. We arrived on location and began the hard, diligent work. The wreckage was truly staggering in depth, and every descent required proper preparation. Half a dozen of us were involved in the salvage, and we used a rather large American salvor vessel that was at least 250 or 300 feet long. We used a SAT system, which is satellite technology and remote sensing, to help locate potential treasure sites and the team's exploration of the ship's remains.

First, they would launch the Snooper from the surface and have somebody in a control panel flying it underwater, doing a search on the wreck. The ROV could get into a tighter space than the Snooper, which went around the vessel and reached the high points, but could not get within the vessel. This is why they used the ROV with a person sitting in the drive, just like you'd be sitting at an office desk. The driver had a row of monitors in front of him and a control panel that controlled the ROV, so he could fly it by looking at the monitors, and that's how he explored the seafloor. In addition to having six thrusters, the ROV had a still camera and a low-light, high-resolution video camera. Whatever that vessel was seeing could also be seen by the team up on the ship, so the coordination of the team was truly excellent. Harvey was the expert with the most experience and was directing not only the divers but also the submarine operator, as well as the ROV operator. The Snooper was pressurized at surface pressure and was not affected by surrounding water pressure, so there was no time limit on it, depending on how long the battery supplies lasted.

There were four divers working at a time. The Snooper submarine wasn't down when we visited the wreck and descended into the dark, cold depths of the ocean. We used a diving bell, which is an airtight, open-bottomed chamber used for salvage work. It is suspended underwater and allows the divers to work and live underwater for extended periods. It works by trapping gas inside the chamber, which is pushed against the water pressure, creating a dry, breathable space. The bell receives a constant supply of gas from the surface.

There were four divers working at a time, two in the bell and two in the habitat. We worked 24 hours, spending about 12 hours on the bottom and swapping out hot water, gas, and cable from the diver to the belt back up to the control room on board the ship. Our bell launched over the starboard side, and we covered the territory just from that side. Then, on a track attached to the habitat, the divers went through from the bell, through a trunk lock, back into the habitat.

When it was my time to walk on the submerged deck of the once-luxurious vessel, I went down an open bell, which was open on its cylindrical surface and on all sides except the top. Lining that bell was emergency gas, so if my surface supply of gas was ever interrupted, I could tie into the gas that was on that bell.

My time in deep water was limited to 55 or 58 minutes, and then I had to go through the four-hour adjustment process; two and a half hours in the water in what they call wet decompression, and then another two hours in the chamber on the vessel. Clearly, this was a complex and rather demanding endeavor.

The vessel was a side wheel steamer; there were rods that connected to each paddle and a camshaft that connected the two, which was the overall width of the ship from one side to the other, and as high up as the very top of the wheelhouse. I was standing on the walking beam, which is the distinctive large oscillating arm of a type of steam engine used to power old paddle wheel ships. It was 260 feet to the top of the walking beam, which is quite a distance.

My responsibility was go down and take a cable that would be a guide, and attach a cable to the walking beam that would support the belt I had ro anchor the cable, the guide wire for the belt, so I was wrestling this cable that went from me to the surface at 265 feet, and it was secured by a down weight, so the belt could use it to transverse from the surface to the bottom. It was just me, nobody else, and no other vessels in the water at the time. I was just about to complete my task, and my limited assigned time underwater was coming to an end. I was getting ready to return to the surface, while the next diver was preparing to descend to my location and continue with the search where I left off.

And then it happened, a fated, seemingly small occurrence that changed the course of the recovery. I took one final look around the eerie darkness. As I looked over, I noticed the purser's office was missing, which was responsible for all financial and administrative matters relating to both passengers and crew, and, most importantly, usually held passengers' money and valuables in the ship's safe.

Since the wrecked ship ended up leaning heavily to the port side and everything settled on that side, the rails in the upper part of the pilot house eventually started to deteriorate, and the Purchase Office fell in on itself and went to the port side.

It was at a very steep angle, and I was on the high side of the walking beam and just happened to turn my head and look once more at the floor, and something gleamed back at me. I suddenly got startled by a golden glimmer on the floor of the ship's wreckage. It was not a fleeting twinkle, but a boldly shining vision of stunning golden coins, calling to be uncovered and resurrected back into the sunlight. It was a box that had opened up and was filled with $20 gold coins, the glorious golden eagles! The box was about a foot and a half long and a foot wide. And the one box that was broken ended up on the deck, where the purser's office was missing.

My heart raced with excitement, and I immediately tried to convey to the team what I just uncovered, which proved challenging. Since we worked at great depth, air's nitrogen can become narcotic, and oxygen can become toxic, so the team used a blender, sometimes called the "scrambler" method, to create specialized mixes that helped divers counteract these issues. They could add helium to the mix to reduce the effects of nitrogen narcosis. We were using Heliox, which made anyone sound like Donald Duck. As a result, the team had a really hard time understanding what I was saying. If it weren't for the scrambler, they would have gotten hysterical from joy that we finally found what we were looking for.

I was trying to convey to them:
"There are coins all over the floor in the purser's office!"

I could have quickly recovered the great find, but I was severely restricted in the time I had on the bottom. So I had to return, do two hours of decompression in the water, and then two more in a chamber in addition to that. It was simply too risky to leave me on the bottom and recover the gold coins at the time. They allowed the next diver to follow my directions on where the treasure was found, and continue with the recovery of gold where I left off.

It was, in fact, the first bag of coins that came up on the Brother Jonathan. And from then on, the mission quickly set a course for great success. There was a great remainder of unopened transfer boxes filled with gold right next to the heap I uncovered.

We also uncovered a small safe. There were two safes in the purser's office, and we found the smaller one, which contained little money and was very difficult to remove from the wreck and bring to the surface. As soon as we got it up, we opened it with a torch by cutting the flanges off that attached from the door to the wall of the safe. There were high expectations of finding the paper money that would have been on board for the Cavalry officers' payrolls, but there was little to be found. The big safe, which probably held much of the money and gold, was never found.

We found 875 gold coins from the 1860s in near-mint condition, and it felt as if the old spirit of long-ago lost travelers surrounded the search area in a heightened sense of an invisible energy charge. This was a quiet closure to their long-lost journey. They worked long and hard for their possessions, and I felt their souls were at peace to see some of their belongings returned to dry land as opposed to remaining forever locked away in the ocean's dark mystery.

It was eerie to stand in that exact dramatic location, where the fatally dangerous unmarked cliff broke the mighty vessel and snatched over two hundred souls out of their bodies, robbed them of their lives, and retained all their possessions. A hundred and twenty-five years is nothing for the ocean. But to the fragile human life, it is an eternity. Later on, when the coins were back above the surface, shining in the sunlight, it felt as if some inexplicable burden, an unfinished event, finally received some resolution to what happened. It is one thing to forever disappear in the ocean, but it is a whole other matter if at least some trace of the perished lives is recovered, so the story shifts and escapes the dark mystery of the sea, locked away in the haunting eternity of the unknown. A historical trace of an ancient story, a failed mission, and forever-lost dreams can remain for people to remember and learn from the past. This way, they recognize their own great fortune and blessings of life in each and every day.

There were numerous other treasures we found, such as 19th-century cut crystal, porcelain plates, glassware, beautiful bottles, tinctures of medicine, and, of course, crates and crates of gold. Each item brought back additional information about passengers' precious lives, their beloved items, what they held on to during their life-altering journey, and what was important to them to bring to their new lives up north in Portland, Seattle, and Vancouver. This was their intention for a hopeful fulfillment of their dreams, and when they lost everything, they also lost their history. A recovered treasure resurrects their memory and stands as proof of their short-lived life, their dreams and efforts that, unfortunately, didn't come to fruition. Such is the sorrow of a shipwreck that claims many lives, and the successful recovery effort does grant a certain kind of consolation. The spell of disappearance is broken, and the traces of lives remain, guiding discoverers with new and valuable historical information. It is very exciting and spiritually fulfilling.

Over time, the recovery efforts on Brother Jonathan uncovered more than twelve hundred golden coins, many of them double eagles. The state of California owns the rights to this historical wreck and to everything located close to shore. It is safe to say that mere miles from the seashore, countless crates of gold still wait at the bottom of the sea, including the large safe filled with precious jewels and gold bars. Two-thirds of the entire sunken fortune of Brother Jonathan's last passengers remains asleep, deep at the darkest bottom of the ocean, forever locked away from the sight of human eyes.

May the treasure stay where it is, and may all the souls that endured that journey feel at peace.

The courage to pursue one's dreams for a better future is one of the most admirable human qualities. Everyone on board the mighty Brother Jonathan had a dream that they carried into the great beyond. Their fearless determination through their final challenging journey remains forever etched in maritime history. The dangerous reef that caught the vessel and caused this tragedy has been named Brother Jonathan Rock as a remembrance and warning to any ship that finds itself in that perilous part of the ocean. So there is closure and a warning, a lesson learned and never forgotten.

Golden coins recovered from Brother Jonathan, Photo by Captain Joseph Amaral Jr.

*Pulling up the diving bell on Brother Jonathan,
Photo by Captain Joseph Amaral Jr.*

Control station on Brother Jonathan, Photo by Captain Joseph Amaral Jr.

Pulling up the diver bell, Brother Jonathan, Photo by Captain Joseph Amaral Jr.

Control panel, Brother Jonathan, Photo by Captain Joseph Amaral Jr.

Water induction vacuum, Brother Jonathan, Photo by Captain Joseph Amaral Jr.

*Glass tincture bottles on Brother Jonathan,
Photo by Captain Joseph Amaral Jr.*

*Ceramic bottle on Brother Jonathan,
Photo by Captain Joseph Amaral Jr.*

*Glass bottles on Brother Jonathan,
Photo by Captain Joseph Amaral Jr.*

*Initials GR on bottles recovered on Brother Jonathan,
Photo by Captain Joseph Amaral Jr.*

*Ceramic bottle recovered from Brother Jonathan,
Photo by Captain Joseph Amaral Jr.*

Sailing Ships and Small Boats in Rough Sea off the Coast ~ 1885
Samuel Owen, English, 1768-1857

Chapter Five
THE HEROES, HAULERS & ENEMIES OF THE HIGH SEAS

An official portrait photograph of BM1 Bernie Webber, U.S. Coast Guard

A painting by Richard Kaiser of CG-36500 in heavy seas nearing the broken stern half of the Pendleton. U.S. Coast Guard

THE HEROES

THE HISTORIC RESCUE OF PENDLETON

LOCATION: *Off the coast of Chatham, Monomoy Island, Massachusetts*
WATER DEPTH: *approximately 90 feet*
DATE OF SHIPWRECK: *February 18, 1952*
CAUSE: *Broke in two*
PASSENGERS: *41 crew members*
SURVIVORS: *Nine lives lost during breakage, one during the rescue mission, 32 survivors*

The SS Pendleton was a Type T2-SE-A1 steel tanker built in 1942 by the Kaiser Company, of Swan Island Shipyard in Portland, Oregon. It was built for the War Shipping Administration and was 504 feet long and 68.2 feet deep. The tanker was launched on 21 January 1944, and the United States Marine Corps used it until 1948, when it was sold to National Bulk Carriers. Her propulsion was turbo-electric, meaning a steam turbine drove a generator that produced electricity to power a motor that drove the propeller shaft. In the summer of 1952, the Pendleton had an incident on the Hudson River, New York, and ran aground. There was some substantial damage to the hull, but they refloated the vessel the next day. The damage was challenging and later played a contributing role in the final accident and sinking of the tanker.

On 18 February 1952, the Pendleton was en route from New Orleans to Boston with Captain John J. Fitzgerald in command of the vessel. It was about five days out of Baton Rouge, Louisiana, when it got caught in a gale just south of Cape Cod. Suddenly, there was a very loud noise, almost like an explosion, when the Pendleton snapped in two, and the ship nosed down.

Since everything happened unexpectedly and quickly, the crew had no time to send a distress signal. In fact, the radio room in the bow was cut off from power in the stern, so the crew was in a very precarious situation.

In response to the distress call, a United States Coast Guard aircraft was diverted from another search and located the Pendleton, but there was a lot of confusion because two tanker emergencies split in half at the same time. This was not entirely impossible, since the T2 tankers were prone to breaking in two, especially in cold weather.

The broken Pendleton was grounded near Monomoy Island. It was the Coast Guard motor lifeboat CG36500 that was dispatched to find and rescue any possible survivors on the tanker. The Captain was a Boatswain's mate, First Class Bernard Webber, a courageous man who led the search from Chatham, Massachusetts.

But despite their best intentions, the rescue was nearly impossible, as the ocean waves furiously pounded the small lifeboat. Once it managed to get over the sandbar on its way out of the harbor, it was damaged and suddenly, without a reliable compass. But they did not give up; instead, they decided to move on and eventually found the Pendleton, along with all the survivors who waited with hope in their eyes despite devastating and discouraging conditions. The lifeboat motored back and forth in a mind-boggling maneuver so the crew could descend on Jacob's ladder, one by one, and jump into the lifeboat. It was pretty scary, but they managed. The space was crammed, but they all came on board, except for the nine crew members who were lost, including Captain John Fitzgerald and a beloved cook who slipped off the ladder and was instantly crushed. Despite other instructions from the headquarters to take the survivors to another boat, the lifeboat's Captain Webber decided against it and took the survivors straight to the shore in Chatham, which he successfully accomplished against all odds. The Pendleton rescue is considered the greatest small-boat rescue in history. What a story of bravery and fearless dedication!

When Arnie and I worked on the Pendleton, its stern section was still visible, but it was later blown as a hazard to navigation. The wreckage of the bow was also on the seafloor nearby, and the ship's remains were loaded with marine equipment and transfer pumps, condensers, bronze, big brass heads, and miles of copper tubing. We made a good plan for our salvage project, which required me to do a little bit of blasting and blowing off wheels. So, we salvaged the three transfer pumps and sold them to a gentleman in upstate New York who still had the ships that required that particular type of pump. They were made from bronze and needed to be separated first, so it was quite a task. It was very fortunate that Arnie had many contacts and knew professionals in the industry who had powerful boats capable of lifting heavy objects off the ocean floor, right out of the wreck. We felt good about being able to recover some part of that mighty vessel that remains in history books for the bravery of the rescue captain and his crew. The ocean and working with ships of all kinds require great courage and demand a fearless disposition to face a mighty challenge head-on and think with lightning speed. I love that aspect of it all and feel a certain unusual connection with the heroes of the past, when seeing a vessel like Pendleton up close, quietly resting at sea, at peace with its memories and proud of the brave men it carried on board in its time of service.

THE WINGS BENEATH THE WAVES

I wish to share with you two other heroic stories that I came in close contact with during my long career at sea. These recoveries were not connected to a shipwreck but rather to another kind of accident whose aftermath landed in the ocean.

There were numerous times when I was engaged in the difficult task of helping with the recovery of the remains after an airplane or a helicopter crashed into the sea. These were no doubt difficult recovery missions that required much stamina and endurance.

But there were two much older cases that, believe it or not, had a happy ending. These two accidents occurred during wartime, and the pilots were no doubt true heroes, flying Navy fighter planes that were likely in training before being shipped overseas to fight in World War II. They both crashed in Cape Cod Bay, where I found and explored the wreckage.

Nobody had ever seen the plane's remains since they crashed in the bay, but what made these two projects a considerably more uplifting experience was the fact that in both cases, the young pilots were lucky and survived.

There used to be an air station in Quincy, Massachusetts, and both pilots were part of a flight wing training to deploy to Europe during World War II. The first Navy plane sank off

East Dennis, Massachusetts, in the Cape Cod Bay, very close to where I lived at that time. In one case, the plane's engine failed, and in both cases, the pilots parachuted out, landed in the ocean, and fortunately survived. It was in the middle of the day, so people on shore and at sea witnessed the accident and came to help with the rescue effort. On each occasion, a local fishing boat quickly picked up the pilot.

In the second case, the pilot ejected quite close to the shore and landed in about 20 feet of water. He safely reached the ocean, and again, the fishermen rescued him at once. Both planes were in the same area, and right after I uncovered the first plane, there was a lot of media interest in the decades-old accident, and even a local TV station did a special on it. I felt a close connection with the two brave young men who were called to fight in the war, and I understood what a profound impact such an accident must have had on both their lives. But I also rejoiced in knowing that they were fortunate enough to survive and tell a brave story of courage to their families and loved ones upon their much-anticipated return.

Perhaps sometimes one learns to appreciate life so much more after coming dangerously close to the heavenly gates, and when given another opportunity to remain in this world, they create a wonderful life for themselves, always aware of how fleeting and precious each given moment is.

*Airplane crash off Block Island, RI,
Photo by Captain Joseph Amaral Jr.*

*Airplane crash off Block Island, RI,
Photo of Mike Cearta and Captain Joseph Amaral Jr.
Photo by Robert Marris*

WW II Sky Raider, Cape Cod Bay
Photo by Captain Joseph Amaral Jr.

WW II Fighter, Cape Cod Bay
Diver Captain Joseph Amaral Jr.
Photo by Arnie Carr

*WW II Fighter cockpit,
Cape Cod Bay
Diver Captain Joseph
Amaral Jr.
Photo by Arnie Carr*

*WW II Fighter
Wing gun 50 Caliber,
Cape Cod Bay
Diver Captain Joseph
Amaral Jr.
Photo by Arnie Carr*

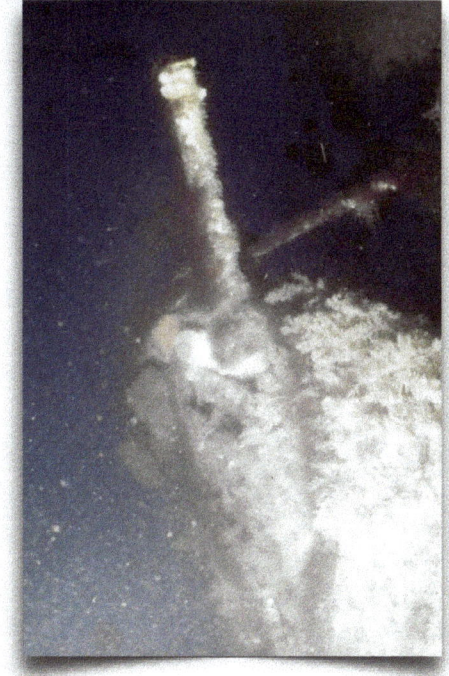

Coal mining in a Mine Shaft, 1923
Josef Danilowatz

THE HAULERS
THE SEACONNET

LOCATION: *Martha's Vineyard, southwest of Cuttyhunk Island, Massachusetts*
WATER DEPTH: *100 feet*
DATE OF SHIPWRECK: *April 29, 1923*
CAUSE: *Storm in Vineyard Sound*
PASSENGERS: *Thirty crew members*
SURVIVORS: *Twenty-three crew members survived; seven lost their lives*

This mighty steel collier - a ship that carried coal- was built in record time of twenty-six days. It was 1918, and the ship was needed for the WW I. effort. The builders were Camden, New Jersey, by New York S. B. Co., and the vessel was initially owned by the United States. It was formerly named Tucahoe and was 318 feet long, 49 feet wide, and 24 feet deep.

The Seaconnet carried a cargo of coal from Norfolk to Boston when it sank in a storm off the coast of Massachusetts, causing the tragic loss of seven lives. Oddly enough, the shipwreck occurred just a couple of weeks after the sinking of the legendary John Dwight off the coast of California, which was another dramatic historical shipwreck.

The Seaconnet was under Captain Daniel J. Miller's command when they loaded her with coal in Boston and departed for Virginia on Friday the 13th. A little over a week after they took off, the weather became extremely volatile, with incessant rain for five straight days. The ship was relatively young, at only five years old, and should have been able to endure the springtime weather challenge. Still, unfortunately, it soon developed a minor leak that became a serious problem when water began pouring in through the seams. It was four in the morning, and the crew was suddenly under extreme duress.

As the ship began tilting permanently to the starboard side, Captain Miller quickly ordered to do all they could to pump the excess incoming water overboard. It didn't do much good, and even when the entire crew vigorously pumped the water, it all seemed in vain and made little difference. After two hours of all hands on deck doing their very best, it became clear their efforts were in vain, and they were doomed. At six in the morning, the men were already up to their waist in water, and everyone realized they were rapidly sinking, which prompted Captain Miller to call for help.

As the Seconnet sent the distress signal in the last minutes before it all went under, Captain Miller quickly ordered a lifeboat that was lowered on the starboard side with two passengers and five crewmen to man the boat. They thankfully reached a nearby Vineyard Sound Lightship later on and survived. For the rest of the crew, it became clear the vessel was ill-fated, so the Captain hurriedly ordered all hands on deck to immediately put on the lifejackets and abandon the sinking ship that began dipping below the water's surface while the wild waves kept smashing over the deck. The lifeboats were lowered, and most of the crewmen managed to rescue themselves, while the brave Captain and ship's Quartermaster John Santiago remained on the bridge until the last possible moment.

The Captain ordered his quartermaster to jump and then followed suit. He managed to grab onto some wreckage, while his quartermaster was less fortunate and desperately clung to a part of the ship that was rapidly sinking. The Captain called out to his dear colleague, but it was unfortunately all in vain. The ocean waves were roaring around him in unbound fury, and all he could do was witness the dramatic sinking of his ship and the harrowing demise of his dear friend and colleague with it.

The steamer City of Rome did hear the distress signals since it was only fifteen miles, away, as did the second vessel Acushnet, which was also close by, but despite the seemingly short distance, the Seaconnet sank with such rapid speed that both vessels arrived too late and found nothing but wreckage.

The Seaconnet ended up upside down but otherwise intact under about 100 feet of water. Captain Daniel J. Miller survived the shipwreck and was rescued and brought to Vineyard Sound Lightship. He later recounted the terrifying experience of the ship's final moments, with a stirring and most famous resolve:

"I will never sail on a Friday and never sail on the 13th again."
Captain Daniel J. Miller Jr., April 30, 1923

It was the great team of Arnie and me that went to explore the old Seaconnet with a sixty-foot boat called the Bottom Scratcher. We scoped the terrain and quickly assessed that the propeller freighter was worth salvaging. The Seaconnet had a big truck-sized wheel, so the task required me to go down and properly rig the charge. We needed to blow the propeller off the big wheel, and since we were on his wooden boat, Arnie was worried about knocking the stuffing out, which could have happened easily.

Being an explosives professional, I certainly knew how to accomplish our goal. While waiting for the charge to blow up, I sat in a small and somewhat dinghy rowboat, while Arnie steamed away and left me there to blow the propeller off. When it finally happened, all was well, even though I felt like somebody seriously kicked me in the pants. Then I went back down and checked whether or not it was off the shaft. Success! I had blown it clean off the shaft, and it was lying next to the rudder. It was quite large, so it was a real challenge to pick it up, since it was simply too heavy. But after a few attempts, we managed.

We also pulled up the anchor, which was quite a project in itself, but with the help of a friend, we ended up lifting it up over the railing and got it on dry land. The ship's anchor always seemed to me like its last warrior, a quiet witness to the tragic end, carrying a sense of regret that, no matter its mighty size and weight, it could not somehow save the vessel.

I collected a great many anchors during my adventures and always made sure they landed in a nice location, usually on display for countless ships and sea enthusiasts to admire. That great summer was filled with countless sea adventures, and we felt good about salvaging the propeller and preserving the anchor of the mighty old vessel that endured such a dramatic past.

Stone Quarry, 1923
Josef Ullmann, Czech, 1870 - 1922

THE HENRY ENDICOTT

LOCATION: *2.25 miles east-southeast of Manomet Point in Plymouth, Massachusetts.*
WATER DEPTH: *86 feet*
DATE OF SHIPWRECK: *September 18, 1939*
CAUSE: *Foundered while being towed during heavy seas.*
PASSENGERS: *Three*
SURVIVORS: *All survived*

The Henry Endicott was a schooner barge that was constructed in 1908 at Bath, Maine, by Kelley, Spear & Company. The vessel was one of fourteen four-masted schooners that were launched in that period of time, between 1901 and 1914, and was owned by Delaware, Lackawanna and Western Coal Co. It measured 192 feet in length and 35 feet in width; however, at that time, the building of schooners was waning, since barges were easier and less expensive to build as well as operate and therefore more cost-effective. A steamer tugboat could tow more barges and required fewer crewmen.

The Henry Endicott was loaded with heavy granite paving blocks that were made in quarries on Vinalhaven Island, Maine. It was obvious that the vessel was seriously overloaded, but the steam tug Nottingham nevertheless took it in tow with two other barges bound for New York. It was manageable for a while, but once they passed Manomet Point in Plymouth, Massachusetts, the weather shifted and became rather volatile. The heavy seas disrupted and separated the schooner barge's towline, so it opened at its seams.

The situation quickly grew dire when the ship's pumps could not prevent the ever-increasing flood of water, and after the crew gave it their best, it quickly became clear the vessel was in grave danger of sinking. They sent a distress signal with rockets in hopes of attracting the Coast Guard's attention.

Unfortunately, the incessant rough seas made it impossible, and the steam tug Nottingham was unable to reach and help the Henry Endicott. The vessel was in dire danger, as the ocean was simply too dangerous to navigate safely. While attempting to rescue all three barges, The Nottingham attempted to first deal with the two other vessels in danger, so it decided to anchor the second one and tow the third one to safety, but this left the first barge, the Henry Endicott, on its own, incapable of managing the continuous heavy influx of water. As a result, the ship sank to a depth of more than 80 feet. But there was a lucky element in this dramatic shipwreck story, for all three brave crew members fortunately survived.

When I took a close look at this wreckage on the seafloor, it was quite astounding to see the large number of paving stones scattered about, with part of the hull buried beneath the cargo. The recovery project was tedious and lengthy, not to mention the heavy weight of the large granite blocks, which posed a challenge of its own.

But with good project organization and skillful handling of the valuable cargo, we successfully lifted and returned to light a large amount of the goods, turning a great loss into a useful purpose.

Where are the granite blocks now? They could be anywhere, decorating a beautiful home, public place, garden, or a building, while one thing is certain, the people passing by the luxurious granite surely do not know the long story they endured, before their final location. But as we know, stones can't speak our language, for their beauty speaks for itself.

Morning after Storm, Mid-Atlantic, 1914
Thomas Moran, American, 1837 - 1926

THE WHITE SQUALL

LOCATION: *Cahoons Hollow, Wellfleet, Cape Cod*
WATER DEPTH: *30 feet*
DATE OF SHIPWRECK: *1867*
CAUSE: *Lost in a storm*
PASSENGERS: *Twenty-one*
SURVIVORS: *One*

The White Squall was an iron barque built in Bristol, England, in 1864, for a Liverpool firm. Its name describes a meteorological phenomenon, such as a sudden gust of wind that appears without the usual foreboding dark clouds that often precede a storm. The White Squall's only unusual warning is the whitecaps on the water. I think considering what happened to this vessel, the name could not be more appropriate.

The White Squall was 164 feet long, 27 feet wide, and had a draft - the vertical distance between the waterline and the bottom of its hull- of 17 feet. It was indeed an unlikely storm that sank the vessel on her journey from faraway Singapore and Malaysia to Boston. The months-long voyage was almost complete, but just before reaching her final destination, the vessel was unfortunately caught in an unexpected storm at Cahoon Hollow, Wellfleet, on Cape Cod.

There were twenty-one crew members on board, and according to reports, a seaman named Evans was the only survivor of the shipwreck. The remaining twenty shipmates quickly perished, but Evans clung with his last strength to a bale of jute that washed him ashore, where a life-saving crew found him. It was a dramatic wreck that occurred because the brittle iron bars used for the ship's structural reinforcement fractured. This was due to the stresses caused by the ship's movement and the water's low temperature.

The only survivor lived to tell the frightening tale, and a few days later, the bodies of twenty other crew members were found and properly buried at a local cemetery in Wellfleet on Cape Cod. The shipwreck was visible for some time after the sinking and remains of tremendous historical value. Viewed as an archaeologically significant resource, it is being considered for inclusion in the National Register of Historic Places. The ship's remains show evidence of the presence of the iron bow, stern keel, frames, ship's windlass, and some of its cargo. The unusual aspect of the vessel was, in fact, the particular cargo of tin ingots, blocks of refined tin metal, rattan, and coffee. It was actually the rattan that was most out of the ordinary.

My dear friend Arnie got me involved in this project as a diver, and it proved to be a surprising experience, to say the least. When we uncovered the rare cargo, we were puzzled until we figured out its contents. The tin was nothing we hadn't seen before, but the rattan was packed in small wooden crates, about 12 x 18 in size, that looked like stacked bars of soap.

Once a container was opened, a bright red color seeped out and spread in the water, which looked rather dramatic. This strange substance was called dragon's blood, a red resin sourced from several plant species. Apparently, the rattan palm is quite common in Malaysia and Indonesia. Also known as yantok or Cythere fruit, it gives the red pigment its name, though it is, of course, not actual blood but rather a natural plant substance used for centuries across various cultures. Historically and in modern times, dragon's blood from this region was used for traditional medicine, as well as for dye and pigment in furniture varnish. Most specifically, it was used by Italian violin makers in the 18th century for coloring the beautiful instruments they produced.

There was one item of particular interest to us. It is called a deadeye and is used for running the rigging of traditional sailing ships. The smaller, round, and thick disc is made out of wood and has a few holes right through it. And since the three holes resemble the eyes and the nose, it is named after them. It was a lovely object, very decorative and well preserved.

Such unusual cargo on international ships from faraway places always reminds me of how endless the ocean is and how every place in the world is somehow reachable with a vessel. It points out the reality that, no matter where one lives, we are all linked, near or far, and that the ocean is the great connector, keeping everything and everyone in their proper place. The ocean rules our existence, in every which way, small or large, for without the ocean, there would be no life.

Diver Captain Joseph Amaral Jr. on White Squall
Photo by Arnie Carr

Diver Captain Joseph Amaral Jr. on White Squall
Photo by Arnie Carr

Photo by Do Mi Nic, Shutterstock

The Pottstown, 1944

THE POTTSTOWN

LOCATION: *Eastern entrance of the Cape Cod Canal, Sandwich, Massachusetts.*
WATER DEPTH: *60 feet*
DATE OF SHIPWRECK: *November 17, 1944, during World War II.*
CAUSE: *Sank due to being overloaded*
PASSENGERS: *48 crew members*
SURVIVORS: *All survived*

The Pottstown was a 195-foot-long, 35-foot-wide, and 19-foot-deep schooner barge built in Maine in 1908. The vessel was not a warship, but a civilian cargo barge carrying blocks of granite for manufacturing. It sank during World War II, but its purpose was commercial transportation and not military action.

On November 17, 1944, while being towed, it foundered in a furious storm, and the barge broke its anchor chain. Its captain tried to send distress signals, but during the rescue attempt, the tugboat's propeller became fouled. Thankfully, a Coast Guard vessel was able to save the Pottstown's crew just before the barge sank.

The salvage operation during the war was delayed because divers were unavailable, but eventually, in 1945, the Army Engineers were sent on location to demolish the upper structures, eliminate a navigation hazard, and help clear the wreckage.

When I dove the powerful barge, I could barely see the rails. The cargo of granite blocks was scattered around the hull and on the sea floor. There were so many granite cobblestones on board that in areas it was simply impossible to see the deck. In addition to all these cobblestones, there was a little donkey engine on board that ran on tracks and was used to haul the massive cargo. The very top of the cobblestones was in 40 feet of water, so it was a mighty big pile of stone. We loaded my 60-footer boat with those cobblestone blocks and salvaged quite a few, so we later used them for landscaping. They were originally destined for New York but landed close enough to their final destination.

A final recovery that was rather interesting and visually a true sight to behold, were two impressive anchors that Arnie and I salvaged from the deep beyond. They were perfectly intact and truly a great find, and landed in a lovely location where they can be admired by many for years to come.

Throughout my years retrieving shipwreck treasures and unusual materials of all kinds, I always saw the anchors as the solid symbols of strength, stability, and hope. If you can manage to maintain a powerful anchor within your heart and mind, nothing in this world will ever bring you down.

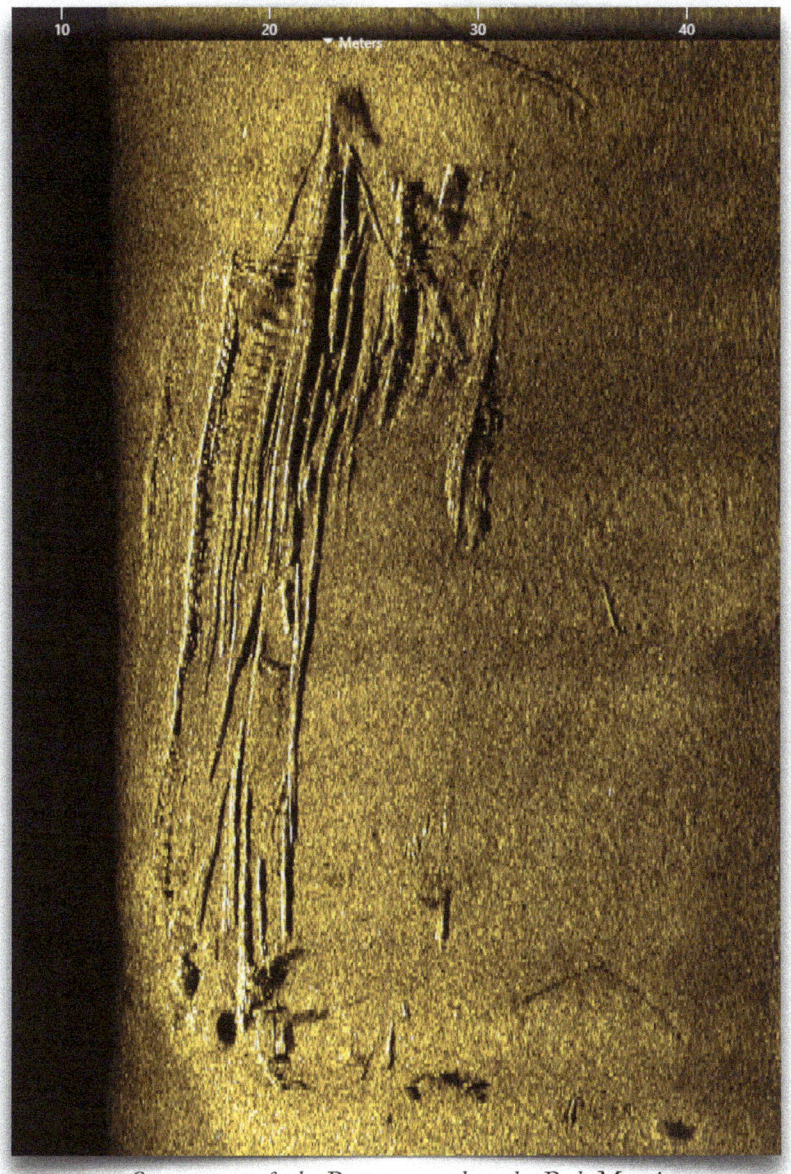
Sonar scan of the Pottstown, photo by Rob Morris

Sonar scan of the vessel Mars, photo by Rob Morris

THE MARS

LOCATION: *Massachusetts Bay, east of Manomet Point*
WATER DEPTH: *120 feet*
DATE OF SHIPWRECK: *September 13, 1942*
CAUSE: *Collided with the tanker Bidwell*
PASSENGERS: *48 crew members*
SURVIVORS: *All survived*

The Mars was a coal-powered steam tug built in 1890 in Camden, New Jersey, and owned by the Martin Marine Transportation Co. The vessel was 117 feet long, 23 feet wide, and 15 feet deep. The sinking remained mysterious for a long time due to World War II. security concerns, and there are no specific records detailing its cargo.

It has been noted that it suffered a collision with the coastal tanker Bidwell, which sheared off the tug's bow. The tug remained upright and mostly intact, with collapsed decking providing entry points to its interior. It is considered a significant shipwreck in the area due to its good condition, offering a unique experience for divers of all levels. Unfortunately, visibility tends to be poor due to a soft clay-mud sea floor.

Years ago, I took my lovely wife, my good friend Rob, and a few others on a diving expedition on the Mars wreckage. After some time of underwater exploration, Rob decided to pop off a porthole, brought it up, and set it right next to the anchor line, which was tied from the Mars all the way up to the stern part of my boat, so the divers could easily surface and then go down on the line and get right on the wreck.

And while my wife was taking a quick peek at this lovely, recovered porthole, she picked it up and accidentally dropped it. It was very funny, as it looked like the porthole wanted to return to its ship. It simply slid off the deck and dropped all the way down into the wreckage and ended up in the vessel's engine room. And when Rob came back to the surface after doing his time on the bottom, he began looking for his porthole, and he couldn't find it.

"What happened to my porthole?" was his question with a very surprised expression on his face.

My wife answered,
"I'm sorry, Rob, I knocked it off, and I think it's in the engine room."

There was a long silence, and I felt really bad. So I said,
 "You know, I can't let this stand. I'll take care of it, and I'll go get it."

After I had everybody back on board, I suited up, went all the way down to the Mars wreckage, went into the engine room, found the porthole, hooked it back on the anchor so that it wouldn't come out, and I resurfaced. I made Rob pull the anchor line, and everyone was happy, especially my darling wife. And let's face it, I would do anything for her, so diving down 120 feet was really a piece of cake.

I would do it again in a heartbeat, because she always was, is, and shall remain the queen of my heart.

*Captain Joseph Amaral Jr. exploring the remains of the vessel Mars,
Photo by Arnie Carr*

Submarine at Sea, 1943
Adolf Bock, German, 1890 - 1968
Courtesy of the Library of Congress

THE ENEMIES
The German Submarine U-853

LOCATION: *Block Island, Rhode Island*
WATER DEPTH: *121 feet*
DATE OF SHIPWRECK: *6 May 1945*
CAUSE: *Sank by American forces in the Battle of Point Judith*
PASSENGERS: *55 crew members*
SURVIVORS: *All lives were lost*

You may not know that during World War II, German so-called "wolfpacks" of U-boats operated in U.S. waters, causing much damage and continuous harassment. This particular German submarine was called U-853 and was a Type IXC/40 U-boat of nazi Germany's Kriegsmarine during World War II. Its construction began in the summer of 1942 and was completed a year later when the submarine began its active service at the end of June 1943, with Captain Lieutenant Helmut Sommer in charge. He was an expert at evading multiple enemy submarine attacks and playing nerve-wracking games of cat and mouse with the Allied Forces. This haunting reputation helped the submarine gain a nickname, the Tightrope Walker.

German submarines generally presented a serious threat to Allied Forces, sinking many ships off the East Coast, in the Gulf of Mexico, and in the Caribbean. These fatal attacks often occurred within sight of land, before the U.S. Navy was able to organize and conduct an effective defense strategy. The U-853 submarine was involved in continuous action during the Battle of the Atlantic and conducted numerous patrols, sinking two major American ships.

On 23 February 1945, Germany sent U-853 on her third war patrol to harass U.S. coastal shipping, under the command of a twenty-four-year-old lieutenant, Helmut Frömsdort. On this particular journey, the nazi U-boat was harassing the United States coastal shipping and brought down USS Eagle 56 near Portland in Maine.
However, World War II was finally coming to an end, and on 5 May 1945, Germany ordered all U-boats to cease offensive operations and immediately return to their bases.

"The war is over" was the command from Germany, but U-boat commander Helmut Frömsdort either did not receive that order or ignored it, and the next day, torpedoed collier Black Point, causing it to sink, during the battle of Point Judith.

Black Point was the last US-flagged merchant ship lost in World War II. Twelve men died, and 34 crew members were rescued. As a consequence, the United States warships USS Moberly, USS Amick, and USS Atherton promptly found the U-853 nazi submarine and sank it with depth charges only eight miles east of Block Island, Rhode Island. To this day, the bodies of German soldiers remain within the hull, which is officially considered a war grave.

I explored this submarine with three of my diving friends, but it was not an easy task. We were tied to the vessel and had an ascent and descent line, while two of us worked together at a time. When I descended, I got quite a surprise when, out of nowhere, a large tiger shark appeared and intentionally bumped into me. Let me say, it was pretty clear he was in attack mode. It seemed a pair of tiger sharks had taken up residence atop the deserted submarine and were not happy about the disruption. So I needed to use a small bangstick, which is a powerhead firearm, for my own protection and to help keep them at bay. Nevertheless, they were pretty fearless and persistently hovered nearby while observing our every move, which was less than comfortable, to say the least.

But we continued on, and once we were on the exterior of the submarine, it became clear that the door to the vessel was tightly shut and locked down with the twisted wheel. After considerable effort, I somehow managed to pry the door open with a hydronic jack, which finally helped open the strong hatch. Some air bubbles came out of the submarine, which surrounded us with an eerie feeling of a dangerous and haunting past. My friend cut the captain's lock, and we entered the submarine, where we observed different open compartments, but for the most part, they were tightly closed and completely sealed off. It was obvious that during the final moments, the crew tried to keep the ship airtight, but with a ruptured hull, this was simply impossible.

The two tiger sharks continued to observe us because we were intruding on their territory, where they made their home. Since we were tied to the submarine, from the bottom of the seafloor and right up to the vessel, every time we would go up and down, there they were. Their expressions and clearly visible jagged teeth made us feel in quite a hurry, so we were eager to leave their premises.

My diving partner and I explored the interior and came upon the captain's logbook. The book itself had a stark visual image, with a black leather-bound cover, and right in the middle of the front cover was the German swastika in bright red. It was all very haunting, I must say. Every time you hold a historical find in your hands, it seems to carry the energy of the last person who held it, and this was no different. The writing inside the logbook was legible, but one could see where the ink bled a bit, and of course, it was written in German, so we could not immediately decipher its content. Nevertheless, it was a good-sized book that had to be turned over to German authorities after every voyage, and since some of those journeys lasted a year, there was a lot of written material.

Soon after we dove that wreck, the word got out to the diving community, and many were eager to explore and try to get into the submarine. Thankfully, the government took charge, welded the hatch back down, and made it impossible for anyone else to get in. The site was declared a war grave, protected by international and national law, and sealed off forever. This was a very wise and necessary decision.

All that remained in the quiet, eternal solitude underwater was the company of tiger Sharks that fiercely guarded the vessel, perhaps with some intuitive awareness that it was best the submarine stays locked and untouched until the end of time.

Ships at Night
Edward Moran, American, 1829 - 1901

Chapter Six

THE LEGEND

The formidable Knight on L'Auguste

Location: Aspy Bay, Cape Breton Island, Nova Scotia
Water depth: Shallow, 20 feet
Date of Shipwreck: November 15, 1761
Cause: Sank in a heavy gale and storm
Passengers: 121 passengers and crew
Survivors: Seven

I have saved my personal favorite story of my adventures at sea for the very end of this book. The L'Auguste project was very close to my heart, and I felt a personal connection with the powerful story of survival, bravery, and resilience of the main historical figure involved in this shipwreck. I had the opportunity to lead the three- year-long recovery process, where we uncovered a unique selection of truly precious and unique treasures. But let me first begin with the powerful account of this historical last voyage that took place almost two centuries ago.

The story of L'Auguste entails the most famous and dramatic Canadian shipwreck. It is definitely very moving, deeply tragic, but thankfully, it also carries a thread of romance.

L'Auguste was a full-rigged sailing ship, constructed from wood and about seventy feet long. It began its life at sea as a French privateer vessel that was engaged in commerce raiding under the commission of war. Eventually, it was captured by the British in 1758 and then shortly thereafter hired by the British government, which finally converted it into a merchant ship.

Her very last voyage dates back to the year 1761, when New France lost the war with the British, and the lives of French Canadians took a dramatic turn. Many of them were sent back to France even though they were born in New France and had never been to Europe. The forced departure was traumatic, quite frightening, for they felt like they were leaving for a faraway foreign land, never to return. But since some of the displaced persons had vague connections with distant relatives in the old world, they hoped for a welcome landing and a possibility of a happy, new, and peaceful life.

The British were in a hurry and quite eager to purge all prominent New France Canadians, especially the ones that held leading positions, particularly figures that were popular and admired, like the Knight St. Luc de La Corne, a well-known historical figure and legendary hero of many battles. Now that the war was lost, he focused on his primary profession as a merchant, in hopes of avoiding a forced exile by the new British government. But it simply didn't make a difference, and he, too, was requested to leave. This was a difficult situation, but there was little or no choice but to obey the British orders.

The departure from Quebec City was set for the beginning of October 1761, and three ships were set to carry the many passengers who were French Exiles and prisoners from the fall of New France. L'Auguste was the largest ship and was to offer accommodation to around 121 immigrants set for France. The Knight La Corne embarked on the ship with his two young sons, along with his brother Louis, who was also a Knight, two nephews, and numerous close friends and wealthy business associates. He left behind his wife, three daughters, and an extended family.

The plan was for La Corne to first establish a new home in France, then return to Montreal to pick up the rest of the family, and finally move everyone to the European continent. The mission was extremely demanding, and everyone on board who had a large family was in a somewhat similar predicament. Since the majority of the other passengers were leaving for good, everyone brought their entire saved fortunes, whatever valuables they had, precious family heirlooms, and a selection of possessions near and dear to their hearts. The ship was packed to the brim with a large group of passengers, including a handful of wealthy and prominent individuals, as well as ordinary families and captured soldiers.

The British captain, Joseph Knowles, was to command the ship, even though the waters around Montreal were rather unfamiliar to him, and he was definitely not well prepared or informed to lead such a dangerous journey. As if the entire situation were not challenging enough, there were numerous complex circumstances that made the journey even more troubling before it began. The British governor, General

James Murray, who was clearly the Knight's enemy, always hiding behind a falsely pretentious smile, continued to cleverly delay the ship's departure. As a result, the weather became increasingly dangerous, as was known in that particular part of the world, where icy, windy northeastern storms have absolutely no mercy, and ocean travel during the winter is simply impossible.

It was late, at the very end of October, on the 28, 1761, when L'Auguste and two other smaller ships were finally allowed to depart. It was not surprising but expected that the ships would encounter severe weather conditions from the beginning. Clearing the volatile Saint Lawrence River was the first major obstacle. To add to the overall dangerous circumstances, L'Auguste was not the ideal ship for this long and turbulent journey, especially not in a harsh Canadian winter. The two Knights, the La Corne brothers, were unbeatable land warriors, but not the most knowledgeable or savvy seamen, and could not recognize the ship's fragile state, despite their raising concerns and persistent requests for a stronger ship ahead of the departure.

Money was no issue for them, and they offered a good price for a newer vessel, but the British governor ensured they had no choice and were forced to use L'Auguste. The governor was simply unbudgeable, deliberately giving them a weaker, older ship so their voyage would be impossible to complete successfully, especially in such challenging winter weather. As a result, the Knights and the entire large group of travelers had no choice but to take a chance and make the best of it. The only assistance they successfully negotiated with the governor was the service of a pilot captain who would show them the way and help them navigate through the most dangerous sections of the Saint Lawrence River. Once they arrived at the Gulf of Saint Lawrence, they would be on their own.

L'Auguste looked mostly fine but somewhat worn on the outside, and certain features indicated serious wear. It was indeed a tired old ship that was previously used in tropical waters, which caused her substantial damage from the boring shipworms. They burrowed into and destroyed submerged wooden structures since they especially thrived on wooden ships; therefore, on the exterior, the damage was hard to detect, and the ship looked perfectly fine, but in fact, it was a fragile hollow shell, barely holding together.

After a few long, daunting stops and delays awaiting weather improvement for days on end, the ship slowly progressed on its journey through the frozen St. Lawrence River towards the bay, aiming to eventually find a straightforward way across the ocean. L'Auguste remained somewhat connected to the two other smaller ships that departed for France at the same time, so they all kept an eye on each other. The pilot captain of the smaller navigating vessel that guided them along the way through the turbulent river left as soon as he could, and suddenly, the three ships heading for France were all alone. However, after a few days of considerable weather-caused delays and vicious, windy conditions causing dangerous obstacles, the ships got somehow separated, and L' Auguste found herself simply lost and entirely on her own.

The Knight La Corne became increasingly concerned when the British Captain revealed that L'Auguste carried on board only charts of the French coast and none of their immediate surroundings, Nova Scotia, or even the western hemisphere. This proved a crucial mistake, for they simply did not know where they were. The more it rained and blew all around them, tossing L'Auguste through the enormous, overwhelming waves, the less orientation they had. The exhausted and traumatized passengers suffered relentless upheaval for days to no end, in addition to running out of food and other provisions. When the storms grew most vicious, they threw themselves into intense prayer, a desperate call for survival.

After seemingly endless days of this agony, the weather suddenly calmed for a short while, and the passengers grew hopeful, finally enjoying a small break. They anchored in a calm bay near Newfoundland, a known rich fishing territory with plenty of codfish. They eagerly replenished their depleted food supplies and caught their breath. Smiles and laughter were in the air for a few short days, and hope returned to their devoted eyes. They believed luck finally came their way, but that hopeful illusion quickly dissipated when, before long, they became overwhelmed by vicious gale winds once again. The brutally helpless conditions quickly robbed them of dreams for a better future in the new homeland. They were not making any progress but seemed to be spinning in the same spot, surrounded by the wild ocean waves, and it soon began to look like their possible chance of survival was rapidly shrinking.

The crew was beyond exhausted, losing their will to go on, so the La Corne brothers, who were well-versed in inspiring leadership, gathered all the traveling men on board, and together they gave it their all in a desperate attempt to help the worn-out crew keep the ship afloat. It was a survival battle like no other, but the storm drove them closer to the shore, which they did not recognize or were familiar with. Captain Knowles was quietly helpless, retreating into a desperate, silent sulk. At the same time, they barely navigated away from the shore to save themselves for three endless days and nights of ongoing winter hell. The persistent high winds, monstrous waves, and furious rainfall hammered them without a break, and they were simply unable to regain some strength for a much-needed recovery. Finally, it became clear that they were caught in an impossible predicament, dangerously close to the unknown shore, which appeared hazardous, with no safe place to land. The visibility was very poor, and they seemed enveloped by the darkest, most volatile, and cloudiest sky.

During this long and relentless ordeal, L'Auguste encountered such massive contrary winds, followed by a Northeastern gale and heavy seas, that it all overwhelmed the fragile ship and therefore badly damaged it. Leaking heavily with an exhausted crew and severely damaged rigging, Captain Knowles desperately sought a sheltered harbor, but was unable to find one in the wild, unknown terrain.

The ship was leaking heavily, and everything was coming to a head, when they noticed a small river's mouth at the shore's far end, and it appeared as if they could possibly navigate in that direction and anchor the ship in the river's bay, where they could stay put and wait out the storm. But as they approached the shore, it became clear the river did not connect to the sea; a dune stood in the way, and the shore was simply too unpredictable and shallow to safely land the big, damaged vessel. The whirlwind of thunder and a perpetual rainstorm enveloped them in the darkest of clouds, where visibility was extremely scarce and their options and hope of survival were clearly gone.

As anticipated with dread, the ship struck land, causing a crushing shock to everyone on board. Panic ensued as the inevitable came and the passengers prepared to jump ship and swim ashore, which was, of course, a certain immediate death. To make matters worse, L'Auguste was struck with a final blast of a sudden, aggressive wind and capsized, which caused the ship's hull to quickly fill with icy water. Everything was chaotic, and despite the crew's attempt to descend a small rescue vessel, it ended up immediately smashing into shambles. The passengers were at once engulfed by the freezing water and gone in an instant, while others jumped ship in a last desperate attempt to save themselves.

They all lost their lives, except for a small group of men who managed to land in one of the rescue vessels that got immediately completely overwhelmed by waves and somehow furiously thrown ashore, before anyone even knew what happened.

In the end, there were only seven survivors, which included the Knight La Corne, Captain Knowles, two soldiers, two servants, and one discharged soldier. They were grief-stricken and hoped they could find and help others, but it became pretty clear that no one else made it. The Knight La Corne was the strongest survivor and helped the others regain their composure and fight to survive. He was extremely courageous, with formidable strength and stamina, while possessing a remarkably noble character. The few surviving men immediately followed his lead and were thankful for his unwavering protection throughout the torturous event.

They waited for a few hours through the long night, hoping that any other survivors would show up, but it was all in vain. Finally, the bodies of others and their loved ones washed ashore, and the survivors had to stoically bury them right there on shore, surrounded by the brutal sea, with death staring right in their faces. The knight La Corne endured a massive personal loss by losing his two darling boys, his beloved brother, and both nephews. His many friends were also taken, and in such a tragic turn of events, one wonders what gave him the strength to go on, but the answer was simple. At home in Canada, he had quite a large number of female relatives, including a wife and three daughters, who would end up in a desperate, dangerous, and destitute circumstance had he just given up and abandoned all hope.

It was a precarious situation, no doubt, since, except for the British Captain Joseph Knowles, the survivors were all French Canadian, now moving in the unknown territory of their newly occupied land by the British enemy. Since the Knight La Corne was very admired amongst Native Indians from their joint battles against the British, he was very capable of surviving in the wilderness. After a few days of walking through icy snow and brutal wind, which pushed them through the thick woods, it was divine luck that the group unexpectedly met a few Native Indians who immediately recognized the Knight La Corne and helped them along. They informed them that they were on Cape Breton Island, in Nova Scotia, in British-occupied territory, not far from the port of Louisburg. Under the guidance of the Native Indians, the survivors came closer to the historic town and parted ways. The Knight La Corne decided to continue his journey on foot and headed back to Montreal through the stupefyingly frigid Canadian winter.

He hired Native Americans to keep him on the right track and help him find his way home through enemy territory. After three months of an utterly exhausting and dangerous journey through ice, snow, and brutal winds, he returned to Montreal and reunited with his family. The British officials could not insist on expelling him yet again, since he planned his return strategy well ahead and immediately informed the authorities and the public of his devastating personal, tragic loss, as well as the loss of all local residents who were the passengers on the fated L'Auguste. He kept a thorough personal diary throughout the treacherous journey, which he presented as proof of the tragedy and thus made it impossible to be expelled. The historical story carries tremendous inspiring qualities of an incredibly brave man.

And what happened to the sunken ship? Throughout history, the shipwreck remains of L' Auguste were very tempting to treasure hunters near and far.

You may wonder why?
The answer is quite simple. Because this time, the rumor that the ship was loaded with tremendous treasures was actually true. When the French-Canadian refugees left Montreal to move to France, they did indeed bring on board the ship all their most valued treasures, expensive jewelry, and gold, all

with the idea that it would help them survive while creating and establishing a new life in France. Of course, when the ship sank, so did all the treasures. Countless artifacts have washed ashore over the centuries, and locals most likely kept the valuables they found. Through the many years that followed, some pirates hunted for the ship's treasures and surely found a nice lot.

Shipwreck, 1850
Francis Danby, English, 1792 - 1861

You might be curious how I became involved with this historical venture. It was around the year 2000, when I found myself up north in Canada through my many travels. It seemed like a sheer coincidence when I became more familiar with the famous L'Auguste shipwreck, but of course it wasn't. The moment I learned about the story and the life of the brave Knight La Corne, I was hooked. It was quite an endeavor that required some serious time and effort, but I was fortunate to find a great partner in Ronald Sirota, who has a significant entrepreneurial spirit and helped us launch this project. To explore the remains of L'Auguste, we gathered an excellent team of highly qualified professionals and worked with the Canadian government to acquire all the proper permits that allowed us to search and work on the excavation for a few years.

I was in charge of the entire diving exploration process, and it was a massive, complex project. The shipwreck territory was actually quite complicated because the ship landed in a bay with particularly complex tides and currents. This caused the remains of L'Auguste to spread over a relatively large area, and every time a storm occurred, our previously perfectly detailed, mapped territory shifted completely. This caused the remains to spread across a large area and made them very difficult to find.

But we did have great success, recovering numerous treasures. We found a large selection of various coins since the passengers carried their entire family fortunes, and many kept coins in different currencies. There was an array of jewelry, beautiful personal objects, shimmering gold, and other interesting artifacts, all carefully sorted, marked, preserved, and properly stored by my friend Rob Reedy, the leading archaeologist and a great person to have on our team. The Canadian government hired him and oversaw the entire complex process of recovery, identification, and proper storage of all treasure finds.

There was one item that I was especially proud to find. The Knight La Corne was a very well-known legendary soldier and was considered the General of the Indians during the French and British War. For all his courageous endeavors and successful battles, he received the St. Louis cross from the French King Louis the XV. It was a special recognition that only a small group of fearless knights would receive. When La Corne was forced to leave New France to establish a new life in Europe, his original plan was to return for his wife and daughters, then take the entire family for a permanent move to Europe. So, he packed all his valuable possessions, including his precious St. Louis Cross. During the shipwreck, the cross was lost, and now, almost two hundred years later, I was the fortunate person to recover it. This was the icing on the cake, and I felt a special connection with the legendary warrior from centuries ago.

Our search in that quiet location, Aspy Bay on Cape Breton Island, generated significant interest, and one summer we had the National Geographic Channel come to film a documentary titled A Treasure Ship's Tragedy, which featured our recovery mission and L'Auguste project. It was exciting to have so much curiosity and appreciation for the project of such importance in the time and place of history.

The ship still remains where it sank that day so long ago, and I presume it will always attract curious explorers; however, not much of value remains there. A display of artifacts from L'Auguste is featured in the Shipwreck Treasures of Nova Scotia exhibit at the Maritime Museum of the Atlantic in Halifax, Nova Scotia.

This fascinating old ship, L'Auguste, and its last passenger's story was my final professional treasure hunting project, and I could not have been more thrilled to finish my exceptional diving career on such a high note. Perhaps because we were both warriors with a survivor spirit, I shall always feel a deep kinship with the Knight La Corne. He holds a very special place in my heart today and until the end of time.

French Louis d'Or - Gold Louis, from King Louis XV era, found on L'Auguste shipwreck, Nova Scotia, 2004
Photo by Captain Joseph Amaral Jr.

FINAL WORD

The reasons I have saved the marvelous L'Auguste story for the end are many. Firstly, this great project was indeed my final treasure hunting sea adventure. Secondly, I greatly favor the story of a brave Knight De La Corne who overcame the impossible. And finally, there is a somewhat happy ending since our hero did indeed survive against all odds and went on to live a long life that positively impacted many in his homeland.

And as you may have realized through my writings, I am at heart an eternal romantic. I love nothing more than the hero to survive, bring home a marvelous treasure, and fall into the arms of his beloved beauty who loves him till the end of time. Perhaps this is so because I myself am enjoying precisely such a life. And let me say, every singular moment of every day, I am appreciating it and remain eternally thankful that the gods have smiled down on me and blessed me in such a generous way.

I leave you now with my final wish. I urge you to discover what awakens your passion in life, fearlessly pursue it, and give it all you've got. The more your cause helps others in need and improves our world, the better. I promise, you will be surprised by the beauty life holds in each and every day, whether in the simplest or perhaps the invisible, unspoken ways. What matters is your true heart's good intention, for in it your eternal soul carries all the long-lost memories of times past. Perhaps you also traveled by ship across the vast oceans, fought heavy battles, miraculously survived, and went on to live a long life that inspired generations behind you.

Life is a fantastic adventure, but it's up to you to take the first step into the unknown. Pursuing your dreams may not always be easy. But if you do, you shall be rewarded, have no doubt. And the rest is, as they say, history. May your life shower you with blessings of inspiration, goodness, and love, so that you teach those who follow what really matters in life most. Generous kindness, everlasting compassion, bravery and courage, unwavering fearlessness, and, of course, unconditional love. It is what makes the world go around, and for as long as we remember and embody these principles, we shall be all right.

Fair winds, my friend,

Captain Joseph Amaral Jr.

ABOUT THE AUTHOR

Captain Joseph Amaral Jr. gained nationwide acclaim when he discovered the captain's ring on the famed shipwreck De Braak off the coast of California. The success of his various shipwreck recovery missions was featured in numerous national publications, including Time magazine. The multi-year project he led in Nova Scotia, which recovered the remains of the 1762 shipwreck L'Auguste, was extensively filmed for the Discovery Channel documentary titled *A Treasure Ship's Tragedy*. Captain Amaral is considered a true expert in sea recovery and shipwrecks and is highly regarded in the field.

He grew up on Cape Cod and became a diver at a very young age. At 18, right out of high school, he followed in his father's footsteps and enlisted in the army. He first attended infantry and then demolition training. Next, he went to jump school and then joined the third special forces group. He underwent rigorous training at a scuba school in Key West, Florida, run by Navy SEALs. He was shipped out to the 10th Spectrum forces group in Bastos, Germany, where he remained for a year and underwent rigorous training, including jumping and intense night operations.

He was on a 12-man member strike force, with the whole team coming down on a levy for Vietnam. Captain Amaral went to Vietnam with the 5th Special Forces Group, where he got wounded twice, but resiliently bounced back and remained there until he was put out of the military after his second injury. He is the recipient of two Purple Hearts, a Bronze Star for Valor, and numerous recognitions for his combat distinguished service achievements.

Captain Amaral was a Coast Guard-licensed Captain and held a 500-ton master's license to operate vessels on the Atlantic and Pacific Oceans.

After an extensive career as a professional commercial diver, Captain Amaral became a much sought-after consultant for shipwreck and plane wreckage recovery and marine salvage, offering his expertise in investigation, deep-sea technology, archaeological recovery, and military logistics.

He continues to consult on complex projects for insurance companies, large corporations, governments, and private client recovery missions about procedures, risk management, and the environmental impact of deep salvage recovery.

Visit the author's website at:
WWW.CAPTAINJOSEPHAMARAL.COM

Upper left row left to right:
Special Forces Airborne, CIB - Combat Infantryman's Badge
Paratrooper, A First-Class Diver
Row of four Presidential Citations of Honor
Middle row left to right:
The Bronze Star with the V Device, Purple Heart
Army Commendation Medal with the V Device, National Defense
Bottom row left to right:
Vietnam Service Honor, Republic of Vietnam Service Honor
The Vietnamese Cross of Gallantry, Vietnam Service

www.ingramcontent.com/pod-product-compliance
Lightning Source LLC
Chambersburg PA
CBHW070737160426
43192CB00009B/1472